Turtle
ON THE
Fencepost

Finding Faith
Through Doubt

RICHARD B. PATTERSON

Liguori
LIGUORI, MISSOURI

Imprimi Potest:
Harry Grile, CSsR, Provincial
Denver Province, The Redemptorists

Published by Liguori Publications
Liguori, Missouri 63057

To order, call 800-325-9521
www.liguori.org

Library of Congress Cataloging-in-Publication Data

Patterson, Richard B.
  Turtle on the fencepost : finding faith through doubt / Richard B. Patterson.—1st ed.
      p. cm.
  1. Patterson, Richard B. 2. Catholics—Biography. 3. Faith. 4. Spirituality—Catholic Church. I. Title.
    BX4705.P37985A3 2012
    282.092—dc23
    [B]
                                                        2012020386

p ISBN 978-0-7648-2203-2
e ISBN 978-0-7648-6723-1

Liguori Publications, a nonprofit corporation, is an apostolate of The Redemptorists. To learn more about The Redemptorists, visit Redemptorists.com.

Printed in the United States of America
16 15 14 13 12 / 5 4 3 2 1
First Edition

Contents

Dedication

To my grandchildren—
Jenna, Cormac, Anna, August, and Eva—
for helping me to remember to have fun.
May you each have the courage to question.

Acknowledgments

I realized a long time ago that one's spiritual story turns out to be a story about relationships. As a Doubter, I have struggled and stumbled along the Doubters' Way. Thankfully I have been blessed with persons who have supported me. Some have even kept me from falling.

This work has been risky for me, given that I am not a theologian or scholar. As such, it was a powerful experience for me when Erin Cartaya of Liguori Publications expressed enthusiasm about *Fencepost*. Her affirmation and belief in the project offset a great deal of fear on my part.

My day-to-day world of working as a therapist is eased by Anna Heredia, who masterfully handles the details of my practice so I also have time to write.

I have been blessed with many fellow travelers along the Doubters' Way, many of whom I have met through my work as a psychologist. Their open sharing of struggles and wounds have pointed the way.

Several friends have spent time listening to me struggle, always affirming, never judging. These companions have included colleagues Walter Allberg and Gerald Bryan; my son-in-law, Mark Miller; and my daughters-in-law, Christine Kunst and Nicole Scalzo.

My children, Matt, Becky, Ben, and Andy, have always supported my search, and each has had the courage to carve out his or her own spiritual path.

My constant companion has been my wife, Pinzy, she of strong faith. Pinzy more than anyone has heard my struggles and encouraged me. Beyond that, though, her loving kindness has perhaps been the most important turtle on a fencepost, giving me a glimpse of what God has in mind for all of us.

Introduction

Somewhere between college and the present, I seem to have lost the faith of my youth. The strong emotions I would feel at midnight Mass on Christmas Eve. The intense desire to serve God. The deep guilt and fear when I would fall into sin. Somewhere along the way I lost that faith.

I would wonder, what happened? At times I blamed the loss on my sisters' deaths. Maybe it was the Jesuits who gave me permission to think and (horror of horrors!) to question the *Baltimore Catechism*. Or perhaps it was because my job as a psychologist brought me into contact with so much suffering. Or maybe the nuns were right. Maybe it was because I went to a secular school after college. I've come to see that probably all those factors were involved. And more.

I miss that faith. That certainty. Knowing where I stood. Knowing that God watched my every step, for better or worse. The warm feelings of connection with the Divine. Somewhere along the way I began to doubt that faith.

Doubts, I thought early on, were sinful. Or at least a sign of weakness. I would occasionally hear relatives whisper about someone who "lost the faith." Such whisperings were tinged with a bit of judgment. A loss of faith ultimately would seem to be a one-way ticket to hell. Yet I had them. Doubts. Plenty of them. Still do.

I have read a lot over the years and have found help and comfort from many writers. Thomas Merton. C.S. Lewis. Henri Nouwen. All men of deep faith. A faith I lack. But one day it dawned on me that each of these men whom I envied had gone through moments of significant doubt. Is it not conceivable that the rich faith they articulated would in some way have only been possible through doubt? In other words, rather than being the enemy of faith, could it not be possible that doubts could in fact be a doorway?

"Come on, Patterson. That sounds like rationalizing," you might think. Perhaps you're right. Yet I keep coming across thoughts such as this one from Rabbi David Wolpe: "Belief without elements of terror and doubt is fairy tale, not faith" (*The Healer of Shattered Hearts: A Jewish View of God*, Penguin: New York, 1990, p. 7). I have long admired what I call Simple Faith. By this I mean not simplistic faith but rather faith that is uncomplicated by too much thinking. Such faith eludes me. I have often felt like a second-class spiritual citizen in the presence of such faith. But thoughts such as Rabbi Wolpe's raise the possibility that not only are there multiple pathways to God but that my path of doubt and question and argument may have a value of its own. Not better or worse than Simple Faith. Simply different.

I have encountered other writers who not only do not apologize for the Doubters' Path but also seem to embrace it. Anne Lamott, for example, has appealed to me because her path of faith seems to be of the patchwork-quilt type. Well-thought-out, to be sure, but typified by an openness to input from several angles and most definitely by doubts. As such, this quote hit me between the eyes: "...The opposite of faith is not doubt but certainty." (*Plan B: Further Thoughts on Faith*, Riverhead: New York, 2005, pp. 256-7)

Thoughts such as those of Rabbi Wolpe or Anne Lamott are saying more than simply, "Well, doubts are OK. Unfortunate but OK." Rather, they seem to be saying, "Not only are doubts OK, but for some of us they are essential if we are to find any sort of faith." How can this be? With "certainty" we stop seeking. Why bother? I know it all already! But suppose the seeking is an integral facet of faith? Jesus Christ seems to have suggested such. He taught in parables, not so much to make things obscure but rather, perhaps, to make us think. Perhaps faith is found not as an end-point to seeking but rather within the seeking itself. And one strong impetus for seeking is the doubt.

"But wait. Didn't Jesus explain the parables to his disciples?"

Often he did and at times appeared frustrated that he had to. But the disciples were his A-team, and he had to make sure they knew what he was after.

From some perspectives, certainty may even be the enemy of faith. Certainty, by the way, is not the same as Simple Faith. Certainty, rather, is the smug assurance that not only am I right but you are clearly wrong! Certainty, in other words, can give us a sense of "better than" and therefore of comfort. Richard Rohr points out the risk of such certainty, saying that "religion is very often a means to maintain our comfortable image of God," even if destructive, because "we feel better with what we know, even when it does us in" (*Simplicity: The Art of Loving*, Crossroad: New York, 1992, p. 20).

Faith is dynamic. So is doubt. Certainty stagnates. Henri Nouwen observes: "Essential for mature religion is the constant willingness to shift gears, to integrate new insights, and to revise our positions" (*Seeds of Hope: A Henri Nouwen Reader*, Robert Durbach, ed., Bantam Books: New York, 1989, p. 46). And then Thomas Merton offers a stronger warning against certainty: "...If in resisting doubt we convince ourselves that we truly 'know God' we have lost touch with reality" (*Conjectures of a Guilty Bystander*, Image: Garden City, NY, 1968, p. 293).

As we progress, I will be suggesting that faith can be enriched by philosophy, a discipline that appears to tolerate doubts and questions a little more easily than theology. There appears to be less of an emphasis on "correct" or "true" philosophy. (Granted there are avid proponents of philosophical positions.) But there seems to be greater tolerance, even embracing, of doubt. And then we have the admonition from Edward Abbey that the sign of "a good philosopher is one who does not take ideas seriously" (*A Voice Crying in the Wilderness*, St. Martin's Press: New York, 1989, p. 1).

This is an important point to keep in mind on one's journey of faith. I haven't figured out much about God to this point, but one thing I am fairly certain of: He/she has a strange sense of humor. As someone once said, God seems to always have an extra custard pie up his sleeve. As such, in our quest we must be careful not to take ourselves or our ideas too seriously because God seems to have a way of throwing us something that punctures our balloon of certainty. Rather than scurry around trying to seriously shore up our punctured world view, it might be better to laugh.

Where do doubts come from? Some may be purely intellectual, arising, for example, from a confrontation with hard science that appears to uncover much truth without invoking divine involvement. Darwin would seem to be a case in point. More recently, however, there have been developments within the field of neurology that seem to be offering scientific explanations for religious experiences. We will return to the fascinating area of neurotheology later, but for now suffice it to say that a scientific explanation of mystical experience, for example, may cause doubts for some.

Doubts more often would seem to come from experience. Something happens in my life that causes me to question some facet of my faith or perhaps to question the very foundation of my faith—a belief in God. Often such experiences are painful, even harsh ones. The Holocaust, the Killing Fields, 9/11 have all challenged faith. For some, such events are enough to justify rejecting faith. For indeed suffering is one of the most difficult facets of life to reconcile with faith.

Some reconcile such incomprehensible cruelty with the belief that somehow the scales are balanced in the afterlife—either the bad guys and gals get their comeuppance or we somehow are rewarded for our endurance. Others will try to discern some purpose in a larger scheme of things. Suffering, if faced, raises questions. It is this very suffering that often tosses believers into turmoil.

There are two images or themes for this turmoil that also seem to affirm the role of doubt in the journey of faith: the dark night of the soul and the desert.

The dark night of the soul was introduced by the mystic Saint John of the Cross. Saint John articulated a series of spiritual experiences that, in modern terminology, result in a suspension of ego, a reaching of a state that sounds similar to the state of "No Self" talked about by Zen Buddhists. The contemplative process at the spiritual stage can include the desire to return to earlier, more blissful stages. Interestingly, what Saint John suggests can impede this desire are what he calls "scruples": "And although further scruples may come to them—that they are wasting their time, and that it would be well for them to do something else, because they can neither do nor think anything in prayer—let them suffer these scruples and remain in peace...." (*Saint John of the Cross Dark Night of the Soul*, translated by E. Allison Peers, Image Books: New York, 1959, p. 71). Feeling as if my prayer life might be a waste of time certainly would seem to qualify as a doubt. Saint John seems to be saying that, rather than resist the doubt, it should be accepted as a necessary step of the journey. Again there is some similarity to the Buddhist notion of acceptance through mindfulness. Rather than fight the scruples, a Buddhist might say, simply be mindful of them.

More recently, various writers have borrowed the term "dark night of the soul" to refer to more commonly experienced "hard times" such as depression. Thomas Moore uses the term to describe a critical spiritual disruption in one's life: "A true dark night of the soul is not a surface challenge but a development that takes you away from the joy of your ordinary life. An external event or an internal mood strikes you at the core of your existence. This is not just a feeling but a rupture in your very being..." (*Dark Nights of the Soul*, Gotham Books: New York, 2004, p. xiv). Such events can sweep away our moorings. That which we thought to be true now seems uncertain. This loss of certainty can be terrifying.

Moore's view of the Dark Night bears similarity to Stanislav Grof's concept of a spiritual emergency, which he describes as both a crisis and "an opportunity of rising to a new level of aware-ness, or 'spiritual emergence'" (*Spiritual Emergency: When Personal Transformation Becomes a Crisis*, Jeremy P. Tarcher: Los Angeles, 1989, p. x).

Another metaphor one may find for a time of serious doubt-ing is the desert. I like this metaphor. Having lived in the desert Southwest for thirty-five years, I have come to see that it can be experienced as dry and barren, almost hopeless. And yet hidden within that barrenness is some genuine beauty unlike anything I've experienced in other parts of the world.

Later we'll talk more about helping with doubts through the gift of imagination. For now, let's consider the famous temptations of Jesus in the desert. What really happened to Jesus out there? He was tempted with comfort, possessions, and power. The point is that he was tempted! If he were not tempted, the whole experi-ence would lack meaning. And so in the midst of being tempted he raised some questions. "Why not be comforted? What difference will it make? Why not become a ruler? Sure would be easier, and I could still influence people." In other words, these moments of doubt and question were necessary to fully affirm the power of his decision of faith.

As Terry Tempest Williams observed, there is no place to hide. "Every pilgrimage to the desert is a pilgrimage to the self" (*Refuge*, Vintage: New York, 1991, p. 148). Perhaps that is why the desert is so important to the journey of faith. Out there with nothing to distract us, we can't avoid our questions and our doubts.

You might detect by now a certain Taoist element underlying my view of doubts. A Taoist would indeed seem to say that faith can really only have meaning in relationship to doubt and vice versa. To use an image, we really only fully understand and ap-preciate light when we also have a concept of darkness. So it may be with faith. We can only truly embrace and appreciate faith if we also taste the fruit of doubt.

And so we reach the point of this work: to encourage you the reader, the questor, not only to face and accept your doubts but to welcome them, even to cultivate them! There is first of all the psychological reality that what we fear only becomes more powerful if we avoid it. Witness the televangelist caught in a compromising position (literally!) in a motel room. But beyond that is the reality that questions and doubts can enrich our faith, can help it to mature.

Have you ever had a dream of being in a house with unexpected rooms? Where, for example, you are walking through your house but come upon a room you didn't know was there? Such dreams can suggest the existence of inner resources yet discovered. Such a room might be the Room of Doubts.

So I am here not just to express sympathy to you because you have doubts. Rather I wish to encourage and even challenge you to seek them out, to cultivate them! I am inviting you to seek out the desert, to willingly embrace the Dark Night.

We will begin our journey into the desert by further exploring doubts so that you will recognize them, and we will begin the task of cultivating them. To get us started, I will consider different views of God that can arise from doubts. Then, to further illustrate the point, I encourage you to cultivate some doubts by examining some of what I call Jesus' Top Ten Unpopular Sayings. "Love your enemies" is just an example.

I then invite you to wrestle with the most likely and most troublesome source of doubts—the reality of suffering. As part of that wrestling, I will explore the importance of arguing with God as a facet of cultivating doubts.

From there I will examine four themes that become more troublesome once one opens the doorway to doubt—gratitude, God's will, sin, and the afterlife—all ripe for doubting.

Tools will be offered to aid the desert wanderer. These tools will include the use of imagination in expanding Scripture and the exploration of the riches of non-Christian traditions. As part of that exploration, I will look at the value, if any, of organized religions to a Doubter.

Together we will explore the importance of integrity while pursuing the Doubters' Way, which will challenge us to cultivate within us that increasingly uncommon quality as a facet of doubting. As we discuss integrity, it may become apparent to you that the Doubters' Path is indeed a way of living.

We will discuss some possible signposts to guide you and will look at a four-part model of spiritual progress that may be helpful to you.

Three fruits of the desert journey will also be considered. The first is the enrichment of one's creative capacity. Then we will look at an appreciation for the mystical. Finally we will consider hope, an appropriate stopping point. We hear lots about faith, not as much about hope. But for those following the Doubters' Way, hope becomes in some ways more central to the spiritual path.

So what does this have to do with turtles on fenceposts? Mary D. Russell has written an interesting novel titled *The Sparrow* (Ballantine: New York, 1996). Faith is a significant theme of the story. At one point, a character is discussing faith and apparent coincidences with another character, a Jesuit priest from Texas. The Jesuit quotes a Texas saying that if you see a turtle sitting on a fencepost, you can bet he didn't get there by himself. This struck me as a great image for my own spiritual journey. I'm always looking for turtles on fenceposts—signs, if you will. But then it hit me. Maybe my doubts are those turtles on fenceposts!

I hope you choose to join me on the Doubters' Way. I've included some questions and actions that may prove to be turtles on fenceposts for you—subtle signs pointing you toward a deeper truth or a more dynamic relationship with the God of your understanding.

Chapter One

"It is not the writer's task to answer questions but to question answers...."

Edward Abbey

As you begin your journey of doubt, I want to offer you two cautions. Doubts and questions interconnect. Some questions give rise to doubts. Some doubts give rise to questions. I may ask myself, "What is my image of God?" And as I explore that question, I find that I know less about God than I thought. Or I may start with a doubt such as, "Perhaps not everything in the Bible is literal truth," which in turn gives rise to some questions about what I read in the Bible. "Suppose the world was not created in seven days. What happened then?" or, "Well, if I can't take the Bible literally, what did Jesus mean when he said all those things about money?" Thus as you consider entering the desert, remember this caution: Don't ask the question if you're not prepared to deal with the answer or the lack of an answer!

The second caution has to do with the impact in one's life of becoming someone who questions. To question is to challenge the status quo. Much of organized religion has to do with power and with comfort. Questioning challenges both. Richard Rohr observed in *Simplicity: The Art of Living* (Crossroad: New York, 1992, p. 20) that religion is often a means to maintain a comfortable image of God. Then suppose that the way we think about God ought to make us a little uncomfortable in some way. Jesus did say, "I come bringing a sword," didn't he? Certainly sounds like his intent was to stir things up, to make us uncomfortable. Annie Dillard makes a similar point in a more colorful way saying that instead of ladies' straw hats, we should all be wearing crash helmets to church (*Teaching a Stone to Talk: Expeditions and Encounters*, HarperCollins: New York, 1982, p. 58). As we will see shortly, there is much about the Christian message that most Christians prefer to avoid.

So if you ask questions, you might make people uncomfortable. And that can get you into trouble. This is not just idle speculation on my part. At various points in time I have been called "a feminist" (I didn't mind that one), "a heretic" (not so pleasant), and, by a member of the Church hierarchy, "an enemy of the Church." (That one bothered me.)

You have been warned!

If you continue to read, then you have taken a first tentative step into the desert. Let me reassure you that it is my opinion that everyone experiences doubts. To some, they are horrifying, a source of guilt and judgment. I hope that, by keeping an open mind, you may find some real value within your doubts.

It's important, here, that I make obvious that I do not equate faith with belonging to an organized religion. For me personally, I have come to view organized religions as different attempts to wrestle with profound questions. In addition, religions offer organized rituals to help us reaffirm certain themes. On that, I find Kathleen Norris' words helpful to explain why I still feel drawn to attend Sunday Mass: "...Like all the other fools who have dragged themselves to church on Sunday morning, including the pastor, I am there because I need to be reminded that love can be at the center of all things, if we will only keep it there" (*The Cloister Walk*, Riverhead: New York, 1996, p. 346). But religion is not necessary for faith. It is simply one pathway to express and perhaps explore one's faith.

REFLECTION: Where, if anywhere, does organized religion fit into your spiritual journey?

So let's begin to stir up some questions and doubts. In the New Testament, Jesus asks his followers a very significant question: "Who do you say that I am?" With the feel of a pop quiz, Peter fortunately gives a correct answer. Notice, though, that I say *a* correct answer rather than *the* correct answer. Suppose this question is directed to each one of us; but not as a pop quiz, but rather an invitation. Suppose that what Jesus was really saying was, "I can be many things to many people. Think about it. Figure it out. See who I can be to you!" What follows are some different thoughts that might stimulate your quest for your own personal answer to Jesus' question. And keep in mind that the God of the Old Testament wasn't exactly transparent. He/she answers Moses' question by saying "I am who am." Not exactly crystal clear, is it? But again, perhaps it can be interpreted as an invitation.

In that sense, perhaps at times God/Jesus took a somewhat Socratic approach to faith. Socrates, you might remember, was a great teacher whose method wasn't so much to lecture as it was to ask questions. His intent wasn't so much to annoy (although he did refer to himself as a gadfly) as to provoke inner inquiry; to find out what one really thinks and feels; to challenge an unquestioning acceptance of an easy answer. So a Socratic approach to faith might indeed include questions such as, "What do you mean by love, sin, redemption, etc.?" And Socrates might indeed echo Jesus' question: "Indeed. Who do you say he is?" Or, perhaps even more important, "Who do you say that you are?"

Founders of rehabilitation groups commonly believed the pathway to "sobriety" was spiritual in nature. Yet they encountered many who had rejected organized religion—perhaps because of unanswered prayers, perhaps because of judgments passed on them. Yet the pathway to recovery was spiritual. What to do? Thus it led to the concept of "the God of my understanding." This offered persons seeking recovery a great deal of flexibility in how they defined the center of their recovery. Over the years, I have heard some adopt the God of Catholicism or Judaism or any number of other religions. But I have also met with people for whom God was a group consciousness or Taoism or even science. The point is that, for these people, the faith they found was unconventional, perhaps, but it worked. As some folks in rehab groups may say, "If your God doesn't work, find another one."

So this notion of the God of my understanding invites exploration. What do you actually believe about God? Or, more concretely, what is your image of God?

A related perspective that can cast doubt on our image of God comes to us from the Linn brothers and Sheila Fabricant (*Healing the Eight Stages of Life*, Paulist Press: Mahwah, NJ, 1988). These authors make the very important observation that sometimes our image of God is in need of healing because it is filtered by our relationship with our earthly parents, especially our fathers or our father figures. Thus, if my father was distant, I may experience God as distant. If my father was punitive, ditto with God.

I'm inviting you over the next few pages to explore and perhaps expand your image of God. I am going to offer to you a few perspectives that may challenge your existing image. Maybe you'll get some clarity of the God of your understanding. Or maybe you'll just get stirred up.

God's sex

Because of the way the Bible is written, many of us see God as male. To question this can throw one into some turmoil. Yet I have found great comfort in relating to God as female. This has opened up the experience of God as nurturing, almost human-like. Interesting, isn't it, that we hear talk of God's unconditional love in this manner; as if we are thinking of a human person loving us unconditionally (many people have compared this experience to the nurturing love of their grandmother).

The image of God as male comes strongly from the Old Testament. The God of those books is fairly aggressive and punitive, traits we associate with men. Famous works of religious art tended to portray God as a bearded, older, fearsome-looking character. But who are we to put such limits on God? Isn't God vast enough to encompass both male and female? And more? What if we thought of God as Henri Nouwen observed, keeping in mind that God doesn't limit himself/herself in titles or names (*Thomas Merton: Contemplative Critic*, Harper & Row: New York, 1981, p. 37). Even viewing God as male/female may be limiting, but it may be a useful expansion. Try this simple experiment. Read the Twenty-third Psalm but substitute "she" for "he" in reference to God. You might notice, as I did, that this simple substitution could open up a sense of nurturance rather than provision.

There is a related issue worthy of attention: how our image of God is filtered through our parents. My father was a good man—generous, enthusiastic. But he was also ill-tempered and, for a period of time, fairly uninvolved in my life. As a result, one of my struggles with God has been to feel a connection with him in that—at least when I read the Old Testament—I see God as having a temper. Just like my father.

My mother's impact on my image of God was more subtle (given that I grew up with the image of God as solely male). But her faith was powerful, and her devotion to Mary the Mother of Jesus may have given me a glimpse of the importance of the "feminine" components in one's faith. In a less positive vein, my mother, when angry, would not speak to me. Thus it is with great amusement that I relate to Joseph Heller's image of God in his wonderful novel *God Knows* (Simon and Schuster: New York, 1997). This novel is a fictional view of King David, whose relationship with God was, at times, strained. At one point, David states that he is not angry with God; they were just not talking to one another. That's pretty funny when reading it, but when you think about it, have you ever experienced God's silence? Are there times when you reach out in prayer only to hear—nothing? And have you had moments when you consider prayer, then say, "Why bother? God is not listening anyway!"

REFLECTION: Take a moment and recall your parents or parent figures. Does your image of God bear any resemblance to them? If so, how has that image limited you? What questions does that image raise?

God and creation

A literal reading of the Book of Genesis suggests that God's acts of creation ended in the distant past at the beginning of the universe. Such a God may seem remote, aloof, uninvolved, somewhat like George Burns' portayal of the Creator in the wonderful film *Oh God!* At one point George/God says, "I worry about the Big Picture and leave the details to you."

But suppose creation didn't stop after seven days? Suppose in fact that it goes on and that we participate? This is not a novel idea, just not a popular one. Pierre Teilhard de Chardin made the continuation of creation a central point of his theological approach to evolution. He wrote that we may imagine that the creation was completed long ago, but that would be quite wrong because it continues still, "and at the highest levels of the world" (*The Divine Milieu*, Harper and Row: New York, 1968, p. 62). This got Teilhard into trouble.

Later on, Mathew Fox also suggested that creation is ongoing, claiming that creation is never finished or never satisfied (*Creation Spirituality: Liberating Gifts for the Peoples of the Earth*, HarperCollins: San Francisco, 1991, p. 10). Mathew Fox also got into trouble.

Process theologians, looking at—among other things—the morality of environmental issues, have noted that it is impossible not to conceive of God other than in continuous creation, in constant interaction with his creatures (Ian Bradley, *God Is Green: Ecology for Christians*, Image: New York, 1990, p. 47).

As a final example, psychiatrist Fritz Kunkel views ongoing creation as a psychological reality. He suggests the "kingdom of heaven" as a static concept (creation was once and no more) cre-ates the tension in which a certain state of affairs either exists or does not exist in history or beyond space and time. "As a dynamic concept, it is a creative process. How we interact will influence us and change us for better or worse" (Creation Continues, Word Incorporated, 1973, p. 27). At the very least, Kunkel's thoughts put a very different spin on Jesus' words, "The kingdom of God is within you," doesn't it?

If I decide (or at least consider) that creation didn't stop after seven days, I am inevitably generating some disturbing questions. If God is still creating, then where? What is my role in God's ongoing creation? Do I even have a role? And if Kunkel is right and God is creating through me, what is my responsibility? We will see later that our answers to such questions will have a great impact on the Doubters' Way.

God and science

As a Catholic child of the fifties and sixties, I grew up with a certain wariness of science. Any science. The natural sciences were suspect because they appeared to be trying to explain much of creation sans God (witness the ongoing furor over Darwin). Psychological sciences were certainly suspect because they seemed to be trying to explain human behavior sans the soul. Some psychological theorists such as Freud and Skinner dismissed religion as something that met psychological needs but had no objective foundation.

And yet science is with us. Our world has changed—even in my own lifetime—in dramatic, far-reaching ways, all because of science. For some, science has made religion irrelevant; much can be explained without the God concept. So if we open our minds to what science has to offer, we run the risk of fostering doubts.

Fortunately, some argue not that science and religion are incompatible, but offer complementary points of view. Chet Raymo, for example, argues that "religion without science is idolatrous" and that science without religion could be even more dangerous: a power without constraint, wisdom, or love (*Skeptics and True Believers*, Walker and Co.: New York, 1998, p. 129). Even more striking to me was the observation he made about the miracles of the Scriptures and saints being an uncertain basis upon which to base a faith. Instead, he feels that the greater miracle of creation is with us twenty-four hours a day, revealed by science.

Some time back, in part through a book titled *Why God Won't Go Away* by Andrew Newberg, Eugene D'Aquili, and Vince Rause (Ballantine: New York, 2001), I encountered the notion of "neurotheology." The authors make a startling suggestion that "spiritual experience, at its very root, is intimately interwoven with human biology. That biology, in some way, compels the spiritual urge" (p. 8). They describe, for example, studies of mystics in meditation and found a biological basis for the mystical experience of "becoming one," be it with God, the universe, "the Force," etc. In other words, specific parts of the brain are involved directly in such experiences. These authors, however, are not reductionists. They are not trying to explain away spiritual experience as nothing but biology. Rather, they suggest that our brains have evolved to the point that spiritual experience has become inherent to our being. For me, this raised the possibility that God created and evolved our brains in such a way that, with a little effort, we could experience him/her directly. Thus the structure of the human brain as well as its complexity has become compelling evidence for the existence of a higher being.

With excitement I turned to that great cosmic library known as the Internet and typed in "neurotheology" to the search engine. To my dismay, what came back were articles out of fundamentalist Christian magazines attacking the concept. How sad! Rather than examine the ideas, some Christian thinkers were rejecting the whole area of study out of hand as yet another instance of agnostic scientists trying to reduce God to something material. This may give you some feel for how exploring alternate understandings of God may get you into some trouble. But I also hope that it raises for you the possibility that following your doubts can take you into exciting, meaningful, and ultimately enriching points of view (again the irony). This is the Doubters' Way, and it will lead you to a more vibrant faith.

The animosity between science and religion has been nowhere more intensely felt than around the topic of evolution. Darwin's theory appeared to be an affront to the Book of Genesis and, as such, has been under attack ever since, even up to the present time. Lawsuits either to ban the teaching of evolution in schools or at least to give "equal time" to creationist theories are still being heard in our courts. Efforts by the great mystic Teilhard de Chardin to find a spiritual foundation for evolution only got him into trouble with the Vatican.

There is a wonderful play written about fifty years ago that is as relevant today as it was then. Perhaps more so. The play is titled *Inherit the Wind* and was written by Jerome Lawrence and Robert E. Lee (not the Confederate general!). It's a fictional account of the Scopes "monkey trial" conducted in the 1920s. This trial focused on a man named John Scopes, who was being prosecuted for teaching the theory of evolution in a Tennessee school. Scopes was represented by the great criminal attorney Clarence Darrow, while the teachings of the Bible were defended by William Jennings Bryan. The play dramatizes the conflict between the points of view of science and fundamentalist religion. At one point the character of Henry Drummond (Darrow) is examining Matthew Harrison Brady (Bryan), who has agreed to take the witness stand. During the confrontation, Brady confronts Drummond with the challenge that something is "holy" to Drummond, an apparent agnostic. Drummond responds:

> "Yes...The individual human mind....In a child's power to master the multiplication table there is more sanctity than all your shouted 'Amens!' 'Holy, Holies!' and 'Hosannahs!' An idea is a greater monument than a cathedral. And the advance of man's knowledge is more of a miracle than any sticks turned into snakes, or the parting of waters!" (Random House: New York, 1955, p. 93)

Additionally, the closing stage directions give us an image of he/she who follows the Doubters' Way:

> "Drummond picks up a copy of Darwin's *Evolution of Species*. He weighs the volume in his hand....Then Drummond notices the Bible....He picks up the Bible in his other hand; he looks from one volume to the other, balancing them thoughtfully, as if his hands were scales. He half-smiles, half-shrugs. Then Drummond slaps the two books together and jams them in his briefcase, side by side." (p. 129).

This raises an important point: What about the Bible? One of the requirements to walk the Path of Doubt is to have an open mind. That includes a mind open not only to science but also to the Bible. How then can we view the Bible? Can it be viewed as a history? Science seems to dispute this. Perhaps if we took into consideration the thought from Abraham J. Heschel that "the Bible is not a book about God; it is a book about man" (*I Asked for Wonder:*

A Spiritual Anthology of Abraham Joshua Heschel, S.H. Dresner, ed., Crossroad: NY, 1990, p. 53). What Heschel is essentially getting at is to consider the idea of human history via the Bible as really "the history of God in search of man" (*ibid.*, p. 78). Rather than viewing the Bible as a historical document of real-world events, perhaps we can view it as a spiritual document of man in search of God and God in search of man. How much would that change to view it as a simultaneous search? Perhaps we can view it as a collection of spiritual experiences, guidance that we would be foolish to ignore. So it may seem ironic then that a committed Doubter such as myself made a decision a year ago to read the entire Bible. We Catholics do not have a strong sense of the Bible. We hear excerpts at Mass, or we may have even taken a course in school or parish. But we don't know the Bible in any depth. And so at the age of sixty-two, I took it upon myself to read the Bible from Genesis to Revelation.

It has been an interesting journey. It's safe to say that reading the Bible has not resolved any of my doubts and in fact has raised some new ones. Yet paradoxically, and in ways I don't fully understand, it has deepened my faith. Here are some random observations:

Much of the Old Testament is gruesome and violent. Is God really that vengeful? This gruesome, violent quality, however, gives me a strong sense of how Jesus' message of peace and forgiveness really was a revolution.

Some parts of the Bible (such as Deuteronomy and Jeremiah) are very boring no matter what mental gymnastics you try to play.

There is great poetry throughout the Bible, not just in the Book of Psalms.

There are some great courageous women tucked away in the Bible (for example, Esther).

People, especially politicians, really do quote the Bible to suit their own needs. Interestingly, for example, the few sections that speak about homosexuality get quoted far and wide, but the parts condemning charging interest on loans don't get quoted.

I finished the Bible and started reading it again, from cover to cover. I urge you to do the same, and take note of how your experience changes.

REFLECTION: Where, if anywhere, do the Bible and other sacred writings fit into your spiritual journey?

Many great minds have wrestled with the interface of science and religion, some with hope of a fruitful dialogue. But it is more than that. Neither science nor philosophy nor theology seems to have made much of a dent in the basic human tendencies to abuse and destroy one another. As Jacob Needleman notes, "Regarded as though from outer space or from another dimension of time, human history presents a spectacle of the repeated failure of great ideas to penetrate the human heart" (*The Heart of Philosophy*, Jeremy P. Tarcher: New York, 2003, p. 19). Needleman's indictment applies equally to philosophy, theology, and science. Each has failed to fully convert the human heart. One need only look at the current level of widespread violence and hunger to obtain testimony to the validity of his observation.

So the animosity between the fields of religion and science would seem to be a tempest in a teapot when compared to the failure of both to heal the human heart. And this in turn raises the possibility that each in its own way has missed something important about God. Which leads us to Jesus Christ.

Jesus' Ten Most Unpopular Sayings

Regarding one's image of God, the person of Jesus Christ is both a help and a hindrance. Christian religions teach that he was God made man. Therefore when I look at Jesus Christ, I am getting a glimpse of God. As a Doubter, I admit I struggle with this and related beliefs central to Christianity. (For example, why did God become man? To die for our sins is the Christian answer. I struggle to grasp what this means.) But let's, for a moment, accept that Jesus was/is God. Everything he said—I mean everything—becomes profoundly important. Here's where questioning things gets risky. If Jesus really meant what he said as God, we all may be in a lot of trouble. So when, then, do we take Jesus literally and when do we assume he was merely making a point? Did he, for example, really expect us to pluck our eyes out after looking at a provocative magazine? I would hope he wasn't being literal there. But if we don't take him literally there, when do we? This conundrum allows many to "water down" things Jesus said. His comments about the rich are a case in point. This watering down leads to more gray areas.

It appears to me that, first and foremost, Jesus was a trouble-maker intent on shaking us to our foundations. Let's take a look at some of his statements that challenge and (to me) seem to stir up important questions for the Doubters' Path:

1. *"It is easier for a camel to pass through the eye of a needle than for one who is rich to enter the kingdom of God."*

Probably the most ignored facet of Jesus' message has to do with wealth. The rejection of that theme has even given rise to a brand of Christianity known as the religion of prosperity, wherein financial success is applauded and taken as a sign of God's favor.

Notice that Jesus didn't say it was impossible; just hard for a rich man or woman to get into heaven. Why? Because money provides many temptations, the least of which is the acquisition of stuff. Money also provides power. And power has the potential to corrupt. The temptation to seize power is hard to resist.

Perhaps the greatest challenge of wealth is an attitude of entitlement that goes with it. A friend of mine, a physician, once conducted an experiment. He went into a store one day wearing ordinary clothing but obviously wearing a Rolex watch. The next day he went in without the watch. He was certain that the sales persons' attitudes were much more deferential when he wore the Rolex. Persons of wealth, then, can be tempted to develop an attitude of entitlement wherein they expect special treatment because they are wealthy!

2. *"Love your enemies."*

This famous passage and its accompanying encouragement to "turn the other cheek" are taken literally by the Quakers, among others. The rest of us tend to water it down. "Surely," we might think, "Jesus wouldn't expect me to love the likes of Adolf Hitler, Saddam Hussein, or that jerk who lives down the street." We also tend to water down his message when it comes to matters such as war. Thomas Aquinas, for instance, went through some impressive mental gymnastics to come up with the theory and theology of justifiable warfare (a concept, by the way, developed centuries before the atomic bomb, chemical warfare, and other aspects of "progress"). Loving our enemy, then, is something we'd just as soon not want to consider (even though Jesus said it).

Loving my enemies is a much more personal challenge. My enemy is anyone I don't like. Worse yet, my enemy is anyone who doesn't like me! Yet these are the people Jesus calls me to love. Am I supposed to invite my enemies over for dinner? I don't know. All I know is I can at least pray that God blesses them, which is hard enough. I remember one time praying for a man who'd given me trouble. I prayed that he'd be able to get a new car I knew he wanted, though I have to admit, at the end of that prayer I added, "At least give him a flat tire once in a while, Lord!"

3. *"Stop judging, that you may not be judged."*

This and No. 2 seem to cluster around a message of gentleness that Jesus often preached about. Yet religions of all stripes seem to overlook this warning. There are two important things to consider in this statement: that religions can become very judgmental and that I myself can be very judgmental. Many persons in recovery, for example, have been very wounded by religious professionals who judged the addiction to be moral weakness. In a similar vein, the classic televangelist points his finger condemning me for my sins yet then proceeds to misuse church funds or hire a prostitute without batting an eye. And lest you think that I am casting stones at others, I also battle being judgmental, expressing my opinion to another driver about his driving, getting caught up in gossip, or any number of other ways.

Human psychology is such that we like to make distinctions. One of the most common distinctions we make is in the domain of "better than/less than." This may be harmless when I make my own private list of the ten greatest baseball players of all time, but it becomes a matter of concern if I conclude that poor people are poor because they are in some way less than me. It becomes a matter of concern any time I invoke some moral high ground to separate myself from someone else's sin (for example, "I would never rob a bank, steal a loaf of bread, cheat on my wife, etc., etc."). But then is Jesus calling us to be morally wishy-washy? That doesn't make sense, either. Perhaps it's nothing more and nothing less than a call to humility and a call to remember to hate the sin but love the sinner.

4. "Take care not to perform righteous deeds in order that people may see them."

Another call to humility. There is no doubt that doing a good deed makes us feel good about ourselves. But what about good deeds done in order to achieve admiration or a degree of power? Is there such a thing as a pure motive? Jesus was clearly annoyed with the Temple big shots around this theme. He saw them making a big deal about their generosity or their sacrifice and believed that their intention was not pure. Everything we do arises from multiple motives. But perhaps Jesus was not talking about motives but rather about intentions. Is my intent to simply be of service or is it manipulative? "If I do this for this person, then he/she will owe me." Kind of like Marlon Brando in *The Godfather*: I'll do this for you but with the expectation that, when the time comes, you'll do something for me, no questions asked.

5. *"Blessed are the peacemakers, for they will be called children of God."*

There's that darn message again about peace and nonviolence! This seems to leave out an important type of "peacemaker," namely, a warrior.

Nowhere in the Beatitudes sermon does it say anything about blessing the warriors. Over the past several years, I have spoken with many warriors, men and women who went to Iraq or Afghanistan to serve their country, to fight an enemy, or simply because it offered them a job. Too many of these young men and women have seen and done things no human being should ever experience. But I have come to believe that Jesus' words about peace are spoken to these warriors as well. To heal. To forgive and be forgiven. To find inner peace and live in peace with their neighbors. To become children of God.

If I as a noncombatant am also drawn to a life of peace, am I called to condemn these warriors? I don't think so. I am called to welcome them back with compassion while at the same time decrying the political and military policies that support war.

Finally, if I am to embrace peacemaking, then I am also called to hold my Church responsible, acknowledging that many so-called Christian religions have encouraged men and women to pick up their weapons and have tacitly, if not openly, encouraged the military industry and benefitted from it. Again, note that the Doubters' Way may make you unpopular.

6. *"The kingdom of God is within you."*

This is one of the statements that got Jesus killed. Think about it. He isn't saying that you have to go to a church or a synagogue to find God. He's saying the kingdom can be found within each and every one of us. In essence, we are the kingdom of God. What a truly revolutionary statement, clearly one that the major domos of organized religion would find threatening. This is one of those statements, similar to "who do you say that I am?" that invites exploration. What does "the kingdom of God" mean to me? How do I understand that kingdom? What is its relevance to me every day? At the very least is it not possible that, if I choose to explore the kingdom of God within me, I might discover what I am capable of and what I am meant to be? And that knowledge in turn may stand in contrast to what I am.

You might also realize that this kingdom is evolving, ever-changing and, as a result, filled with questions and doubts. Your own kingdom within (because it is within) is much the same, changing and evolving in uncertainty through each lived experience. In fact, there may be little about it that is certain.

7. *"(He) causes rain to fall on the just and the unjust."*

Given that rain is sometimes a good thing (for example, in the arid Southwest) and sometimes not a good thing (such as in low-lying flood areas), this means that not only do bad things happen to good people but also that good things happen to bad people. Some tend to cope with these imbalances by expecting justice in the next life. In other words, the suffering will have their reward while the unjust will get their comeuppance. Others, however, would still like an explanation. I once asked one of my clients if she was angry with God. She responded, "No, but I'd sure like to have a peek at his operations manual." Sometimes when life isn't fair, we may be called to trust God. But we can still ask, "why?"

A related reality is that, despite what Hollywood would like us to believe, sometimes the bad guys do get away with it and the good guys suffer. From schoolyard bullies to crooked politicians to overpaid executives, fairness does not always reign. We Doubters have to find some way to live with this. Doubters such as me can only do so by allowing an ongoing argument with the God of our understanding. The only way to trust in what seems unfair is to ask and wait; to argue and wait. After all, it's a journey of faith.

8. *"All who take the sword will perish by the sword."*

My own opinion about this is that Jesus wasn't talking so much about the frontline military grunts but more about the politicos who put them there. In any case, this is yet another of Jesus' statements apparently calling us to a peaceful lifestyle. Sadly, it has been taken as justification for war and killing. I recall, for example, a scene from the beautiful film *Joyeux Noel*, in which a priest is taken to task by his bishop for celebrating a Mass with soldiers from Germany, France, and Scotland. The bishop then preaches to soldiers about to enter battle and exhorts them to kill Germans, reminding them that Jesus came bearing a sword. Is that really what Jesus had in mind?

What I have come to see is that Jesus' message is not a popular one, and to espouse it in a nonselective manner is likely to cause division, even between loved ones. The sword he spoke of also slices religious communities, causing questioning and demands for accountability. That sword slices communities, causing some to speak out about discrimination of marginalized groups such as immigrants and persons of a different sexual identity.

9. *"It is written 'My house shall be called a house of prayer' but you are making it a den of thieves."*

It's hard to see how this statement reconciles with Friday-night bingo. It's also hard to reconcile this with the reality that, within my own Catholic Church, parishes are becoming corporations to protect financial interests. And it is especially hard to reconcile this statement with evidence of opulence in churches and preachers.

The parish to which I belong started out as a small group that met on the basketball court of the nearby junior high school. I liked that. There was intimacy and simplicity. But growth was the theme of the day; more parishioners and more money. As such, the pastor and council eventually decided to build a church. It may as well have come right out of the film *Field of Dreams*: "If you build it, they will come," because that is exactly what happened.

I suppose it is naïve of me to long for the days of the basketball court. But I do wonder if we are getting it wrong by building and building. And as I leave Mass amidst bake sales and tickets to dances, I wonder if indeed we have become a den of thieves. If he were to show up there, I wonder if Jesus would be turning over the cupcake tables and chasing after the people raffling off a fancy automobile at $200 a chance.

10. *"It is I. Do not be afraid."*

From a Christian perspective, this is the essence of "let go and let God." Jesus is apparently inviting us to put our complete trust in him and to let go of all the different controlling behaviors, big and small, which we use daily. I don't believe he encourages us to abrogate responsibility. I once was sitting in a support meeting and someone announced, "I got fed up with my boss, so I quit my job. I'm turning it all over to God." I had a problem with that, given that I don't believe God runs an employment agency. So it is an ongoing challenge to relate to this statement of Jesus. Many would just as soon ignore it. In my own case, this is an area where my doubts cause me trouble. When I think, "Just let go and let God," fear kicks in. Suppose no one is there! Like Peter, I start sinking into the water!

You might want to come up with your own list of troublesome sayings of Jesus or, for that matter, of any other religious leaders such as Buddha, Muhammad, etc. But don't view them as some sort of intellectual inconsistencies you've discovered. Instead, embrace them as challenges to your own journey. The challenge to embrace your questions and doubts, then, is more than an invitation to exercise being obstinate. It appears to me that one of the greatest of spiritual dangers is to settle into complacency. Finding a comfort zone is some people's functional basis of faith. Sadly, many religions reinforce that tendency. Jacob Needleman (*Heart of Philosophy*) observed that most of our questions are educated out of us by the time we "reach so-called maturity" (*ibid.*, p. 85). The temptation here is to settle for what Dietrich Bonhoeffer and others have called "cheap grace." Essentially, Bonhoeffer criticized churches and churchgoers for settling for "cheap grace," that is, a good feeling with minimal effort and no suffering. Doubters looking for quick answers are seeking cheap grace.

When we question, our faith is alive, vibrant, even passionate. Perhaps this is what we are called for—to be spiritually unsettled, unsure, seeking, questioning. If we stop questioning and doubting, that is when our faith is in real trouble. So to come full circle, when Jesus says to me, "Who do you say that I am?" it appears my answer runs along the lines of, "I don't rightly know. But I sure want to find out! And I am willing to struggle to do so."

Chapter Two

"We're Easter people living in a Good Friday world."

ANNE LAMOTT

When I was two years old, my four-month-old sister died of spina bifida. I had already had an older sister die of the same disease. These two children would come to play an important role on my own spiritual journey, for I would find, even at a young age, that I didn't quite understand why such tragedy had struck my family. My mother's stoic belief in God's will didn't work for me. And so I would privately question. And when I heard sermons about a loving God, I would doubt.

REFLECTION: Have you had experiences of pain that threw you into a state of doubt or questioning? In other words, when have you struggled with the question, "Why?"

In the spirit of encouraging thoughtful questioning in this most difficult area, let us examine some of the more common views of suffering.

Most discussions of suffering make a distinction between suffering at the hands of others or suffering via natural disasters. But the key ingredient in both is free will. God gave us free will, goes the thinking. Therefore, we can choose to do evil or not, and others may suffer as a result, or not. While this may have some philosophical appeal, it is rarely a comfort, especially to those who believe that God can intervene in human affairs and protect us. So let's just work with the notion that bad things happen to good people, whether or not as a result of the free will of our fellow human beings.

What does seem to be universally agreed upon is that we may not always have a choice in what happens to us, but we do have a choice in how we will face misfortune. This concept has been around for centuries. The Roman Stoic philosopher Epictetus, for example, wrote that "we cannot choose our external circumstances, but we can always choose how to respond to them" (*The Art of Living*, translated by Sharon Lebell, HarperCollins: San Francisco, 1995, p. 10). More recently, psychiatrist Viktor Frankl made a similar point that became the heart of his brand of therapy known as logotherapy. He states that we are not free from conditions—biological, psychological, or sociological. But we are, he says, free to take a stand toward these conditions, for we have the freedom to choose our attitude toward them (*Psychotherapy and Existentialism*, p. 3). As a survivor of the Holocaust, Frankl speaks with the authority of one who knows suffering. Phillip Simmons, in the midst of coping with Lou Gehrig's disease, spoke of "learning to fall" by which he referred to learning to live richly in the face of loss (*Learning to Fall: The Blessings of an Imperfect Life*, Bantam: New York, 2002, p. xi). These writers, among others, have challenged us to think about how we face senseless suffering.

REFLECTION: How have you tried to face senseless suffering in your life?

While there are those (as above) who focus on how to face senseless suffering, some of course take the position that nothing makes sense; that, in essence, shit happens. They would agree with only half of Forrest Gump's philosophy, viewing all of us as feathers bandied about by the wind. Such a view borders on the edge of despair. In the end, this is why people turn to God to try to make sense of things.

There is the point of view that our suffering exists as punishment for our sins. This would seem to be the point of view of the Old

Testament where God inflicts floods, fire, and brimstone when he gets fed up with our sinning. He also causes pain when some do not follow his game plan. Such a one was Jonah, swallowed by the whale after resisting God's plan for him to become a prophet. As Joseph Telushkin points out, some have invoked this explanation of punishment to account for the Holocaust [a position, by the way, that Telushkin vigorously refutes] (*Jewish Literacy*, Harper-Collins: New York,1991, pp. 609–611). More recently, that line of thought was invoked to account for the AIDS epidemic, again an offensive line of thought.

How much weight you apply to the punishment explanation depends—to some extent—on how punitive the God of your understanding is. The problem that many of us find with this explanation is that it appears to be inconsistent: Not only are very good people punished but some evil people seem to thrive!

This explanation would nonetheless seem to account for at least some of our suffering, namely that part of our suffering that arises as a consequence of our own choices. I have asthmatic lungs. It is tempting in the midst of not being able to breathe to complain, "Why me, God?" The problem is I know why me. I have asthma because earlier in my life I smoked three packs of cigarettes a day! So my bad lungs are a direct result of bad choices I made. Being human, we don't like to acknowledge such responsibility, at times wanting to shift the blame to other human beings or even to God. Thus, the punishment explanation for suffering challenges us to examine our own responsibility in our suffering.

Related to the line of thought regarding punishment explanation, we examine Buddhism's approach to suffering. Here we encounter the belief that our suffering is brought on by our attachments. In other words, the more we are attached to something—be it material possessions, image of ourselves, etc.—when we lose that something, we suffer.

REFLECTION: Is any of your suffering a direct result of choices you made? Do you notice any suffering because of the attachments you are holding onto? What are those attachments?

A second common explanation for the reason for suffering is the notion of God's will. This shows up in a variety of forms, such as my mother's explanation of crosses to bear or the notion of God loading us up with as much as we can handle. God's will may or may not include punishment. How do we know? Or can we? When we say our suffering is part of God's will for us, we are saying there is some reason for this suffering that may not necessarily include punishment for our sins. Perhaps this is left a mystery to gain trust in God. Perhaps there is a lesson waiting to be learned. This would seem to overlap Frankl's idea that meaning can be found in the midst of senseless suffering. Yet the line of thinking that reasons our suffering to God's will goes a step further than Frankl, though, by indicating that the meaning we find is part of the reason why God gave us the suffering in the first place.

A broader version (I will refer to this as the Big Picture) of the God's-will theme suggests there is a much broader picture of the way of things are and that this way is known only to God. Harold S. Kushner, in his justly loved *When Bad Things Happen to Good People*, uses the image of a tapestry. We see the back of the tapestry and so see only loose-dangling threads. But God sees the front of the tapestry (and, in fact, designed it). He sees the pattern. Unfortunately some of us traveling the Doubters' Way are not content with that and, if it's true, want nonetheless to see and understand the pattern.

This point of view finds a parallel in Taoism, which posits the interconnection of opposites. For example, light has no meaning without the existence of dark. Virtue has no meaning without the existence of sin. Such "tension of opposites" cannot be explained but merely tolerated. Daniel Schwartz makes this point with a poetic image that applies to suffering: "...slicing the thorns off the stem shortens the life of the flower" (*Finding Joy: A Practical Spiritual Guide to Happiness*, Jewish Lights: Woodstock, VT, 1996, p. 167).

Another bit of support or possible explanation for the Big Picture theory comes from systems theory, which posits that a given system means more than the sum of its component parts. The human body is an example. The human body would be the pattern tapestry while the various organs, bones, etc., would be the individual strings.

A more recent line of thought suggests that perhaps God is not in charge of everything, that indeed some things "just happen." Anne Lamott, for example, suggests that God's purpose is not to take away our suffering or our pain but rather "to fill it with his or her presence" (*Traveling Mercies: Some Thoughts on Faith*, New York: Pantheon Books, 1999, p. 241). This point of view is certainly a comfort. God didn't will this terrible tragedy or that one. It just happened; but God is here weeping with me. Yet, in the midst of God's presence, the question still arises of where does one draw the line? Where does God stop and everything that is not God's doing start?

REFLECTION: What are your own questions about where God has been in the midst of your suffering?

So again we come back to our image of God. If we see God as all-powerful but not necessarily all-loving (for instance, the Old Testament God), then we may be inclined to view tragedy as punishment. If we see God as all-powerful and all-loving, the problem becomes more difficult. How can a loving God do or permit such tragedies? Free will explains some of this, but we are still left with a great amount of tragedy that is hard to understand if we see God as loving.

The Big Picture explanation ultimately leaves us dependent on an afterlife to at least even the score much less make sense of things. As Joseph Telushkin says, "the only possible explanation for…so much suffering and injustice" being permitted by God "is that in another dimension of existence…there is redress" (*Jewish Wisdom, op. cit.,* p. 276). But then what of the forgiveness of a loving God? Even the concept of hell has trouble squaring with a loving God.

So you can see how a Doubter can get tangled up in knots with this very tricky question of suffering. Nonetheless, some people find comfort in the above explanations. Not answers but comfort. And that's a good thing. The "heavy crosses" theme was a comfort to my mother; that, and the thought that my sisters are now angels. But what about those of us who find no comfort in the available answer and instead are angry? What then?

I have had many well-meaning people tell me that I am wrong to be angry with God. That makes me angry! As I noted earlier, I grew up with the notion that anger was bad and should not be expressed. What I came to see, especially through marriage, is that the withholding of anger tends to create a wider gap than the effort to express it and work through whatever the issue might be. Henri Nouwen echoes this when he discusses our relationship with God, saying we cannot only relate to God in terms of submission. In fact, we are much less distant from God when we "feel free to question divine decrees" (*Seeds of Hope: A Henri Nouwen Reader,* Robert Durbach, ed., Bantam Books: New York, 1989, p. 79). As in our human relationships, the gap between God and ourselves can be lessened with the openness to question and to communicate openly. Pierre Wolff touches directly on this point, referring in *May I Hate God?* to the experience of friendship. His point, in essence, is that in our friendships and loves we experience times of frustration, anger, disappointment, and resentment. If they persisted, we risk having our injured love explode into hatred.

Thus, the only way "to overcome this risk is to express feelings of hatred openly" (*May I Hate God?* Paulist Press: Mahwah, NJ, 1979, p. 15). So it must be, argues Wolff, in our relationship with God.

This may be a part of the Doubters' Way that you do not like. But the path cannot be strictly intellectual. Our whole being needs to be engaged, which includes our emotions. Being angry with God and arguing with him/her is not bad (or wrong). For some on the Doubters' Way, it keeps them connected and in dialogue with God. Still not sure? Then let's turn to the book in the Bible that gives us permission to be angry: the Book of Job.

Most people know the story of Job's suffering and his outcries. But what many people overlook is the troublesome prologue. It seems that Job's difficulties arose out of a bet. God and Satan are having a discussion about faith and God points out Job as a man of faith and honor. Satan retorts that faith is easy when everything in one's life is going well. (Point well-taken!) So God lets Satan persecute Job, insisting only that Job not be killed in the process. Job of course is not clued in on the bet, so when his life falls completely apart, he vents his anger on God. It could be, though, that he would have been angrier if he knew about the bet! As the story unfolds, Job gets no help. His wife encourages him to turn on God. His buddies conclude that he must have sinned in some secret way. In the midst of his misery, Job neither rejects his faith nor judges himself. He simply wants to know why.

There has been much written about Job, in part because it is that part of Scripture which directly addresses the great question of human suffering. I would encourage anyone on the Doubters' Path to read it. But you won't find an answer!

In his excellent book about Job, William Safire (*The First Dissident: The Book of Job in Today's Politics,* Random House: New York, 1992) notes that in around Job's time, if you as my neighbor were bothering me in some way, I could go to a court and demand that you show up and explain yourself. So that's what Job does.

He demands that God show up and explain himself/herself! And God shows up! At this point, some Doubters will be disappointed. God neither apologizes ("You see, Job, I made this bet...") nor gives a clear answer to Job's "why." Instead he/she puts Job in his place. God goes through a fairly poetic listing of everything he's in charge of, suggesting that Job's puny protest is out of line in comparison. However (and this is important), God does not punish Job for his protest. He restores Job to his lifestyle. So, at the very least, it is possible that the Book of Job represents God's permission for us to be angry with him/her.

But as I noted above, the Book of Job offers no solution to the question of suffering. Safire and others have noted that Job is apparently comforted by God's merely showing up. However, Telushkin, based on his own experience, notes that God's showing up for Job makes the issue more complicated for those who suffered through, for example, the Holocaust. If God showed up for Job, why didn't he/she show up in some equally dramatic manner to at least comfort those who survived the Holocaust?

In any case, I would hope that, if you feel drawn to the Doubters' Way, you will allow yourself to argue with the God of your understanding, even to be angry with him/her. Such wrestling creates the potential to generate and enrich your faith.

REFLECTION: Have you ever been/are you now angry with God? How have you dealt with that anger?

I have no idea why bad things happen to good people and good things happen to bad people. Perhaps I never will. That doubt has been a cornerstone of my spiritual quest. One thing I have learned in the process is the spiritual equivalent of the old athletic dictum, "No pain, no gain." It does not seem possible to grow spiritually and psychologically without suffering. There is no resurrection without a crucifixion.

Chapter Three

*"Some people should worry about where they're spending
eternity rather than telling other people to go there!"*

(SPOKEN TO THE AUTHOR BY SISTER ME, SEVENTH GRADE)

If you've ever attended any sort of Twelve-Step meeting, then
you likely have encountered the phrase "attitude of gratitude." With its spiritual emphasis, these groups and their offshoots
recognize the power of gratitude in short-circuiting a variety of
unproductive attitudes, such as resentment and self-pity. Even more
important, gratitude (genuine, heartfelt gratitude) prevents the
arising of something deadly to relationships—taking for granted.

So far so good. No problems for Doubters, right? But at some
point, you may encounter the idea that we should be grateful for
everything in our lives, even the suffering! In these meetings,
one may hear the words "grateful alcoholic," a phrase intended
to reflect the somewhat Taoist awareness that the person in recovery would not have reached a place of serenity without first
experiencing the brokenness.

However, an attitude of gratefulness for suffering and tragedy,
for some of us, seems to border on a scene from *National Lampoon's
Animal House*. Kevin Bacon is being hazed by a campus fraternity.
He gets down on all fours and is swatted on his behind. After each
swat, he thanks the spanker and asks for another. David Stendl-
Rast puts it more seriously and in a manner far more troubling in
Gratefulness: The Heart of Prayer, when he makes the observation that
God has a way of putting time bombs into pretty packages. For a
person to say "thank you" and mean it shows courage (*Gratefulness:
the Heart of Prayer*, Paulist: New York, 1984, p. 104–105).

Have you ever been given a gag gift? Like one of those counterfeit cans of potato chips? You open it and, instead of chips inside, out jumps one of those coiled-up pretend snakes? Imagine that's the case with some of God's actions in our lives. Another way of putting it is the well-worn phrase, "Be careful what you pray for. You just might get it!"

Clearly the issue of gratitude overlaps the question of suffering considered in the previous chapter. Am I to accept everything God dishes out with a smile plastered to my face? If not, then where does gratitude stop and outcry begin? Similarly, the theme of gratitude overlaps our image of God. If my God is all-powerful, then presumably he/she is responsible for everything that happens in my life. Gratitude and outcry then, if that's the case, are at a constant tension. But if God isn't in charge of everything, then to whom am I grateful or to whom do I protest? Take the lottery, for instance. There is no doubt that every week in various parts of the world millions of people deal with yet another unanswered prayer. "I didn't win the lottery!" Yet some people do win the lottery. If they prayed, then how come they won and not me? If they didn't pray, even more so how come!? Or suppose God has no interest in the lottery and therefore has nothing to do with the outcome?

We have focused so far on God's part of the relationship—who we think God is, what responsibility he/she has in the good and bad things that happen in our lives and so forth. But for Doubters there are equally troublesome themes on the part of the equation that has to do with us and our responsibilities.

A dear friend once said, "You can pray all day for potatoes, but you still have to go out and hoe the garden." This whimsical statement reflects the belief that, whether or not God is in charge, we must, at least, cooperate to generate a certain outcome. Yet others would say that God merely offers opportunities; we shape the outcome. A key question then is, "For what am I responsible in my life?" Some New Agers would have us believe that we are responsible for everything, even our diseases. Others would have us believe that everything is predetermined, even our ultimate spot in eternity. So if something good happens in your life, do you give yourself any credit or give all the credit to God? It might seem appealing to give all the credit to God, but then what do we do with the tragic stuff? Some of us have a tendency to give God credit for the good stuff but blame ourselves for the bad. This seems unbalanced. Giving God all the credit has a dark side. It is known as playing the victim. If I feel in charge of nothing, then tragic events can indeed predispose me to think as a victim.

REFLECTION: How do you address and experience the tension around responsibility? In other words, for what is God responsible in your life and for what are you responsible?

Beyond that, how I think about responsibility overlaps with my beliefs about proper conduct. Thus we now turn our attention to the issues of afterlife and sin.

While my early faith included moments of great comforting emotion where I felt very close to the God of my understanding at that time, I have to also admit that fear was constantly present (not so much fear of God but rather fear of hell).

The Church in my youth paid a lot of attention to hell, so that our motivation relied not so much on the desire to be with God but rather on the desire to avoid hell. Every time I burnt my finger or stayed out in the sun too long, I'd think, "This is a glimpse of what it will be like!" We would hear about hell in terrifying detail. And this was long before I encountered Dante's Inferno!

Heaven, on the other hand, held out a strong longing. In various ways, heaven was portrayed as a blissful place (although our youthful theological discussions could never figure out what exactly one did in heaven). In any case, it offered the promise of being reunited with loved ones who were gone. Never having met my grandmothers or my two sisters, this had great appeal. Now that my parents and other loved ones are also gone, it holds even more appeal. The problem is, I'm not sure it's all true! Another stumbling block along the Doubters' Way!

The other powerful role of believing in an afterlife has to do with justice. For some, the existence of the afterlife is what gives meaning to our suffering; the scales will be balanced in the next life. My suffering will be eliminated and I will be rewarded for keeping faith in the face of that suffering. Additionally, those who have caused my suffering will be held accountable.

The Hindu concept of karma operates off a similar notion of justice. In this case, my suffering is my own fault, a result of sinful patterns in previous lives. The afterlife isn't so much a place where the scales are balanced but rather a realm of existence I must earn by living a progressively more virtuous life.

More recent views of an afterlife definitely water things down and eliminate any notion of justice. Such notions suggest that we live on by becoming a part of the whole again. My uniqueness, my individuality dies but that within me which is connected with all of existence goes on. This view is suggested poetically with the closing words of Norman Maclean's *A River Runs Through It*, that eventually all things merge into one and a river runs through it.

There is a certain comfort with such a line of thought, but most of us cling to a longing for a more personal existence in the afterlife, including the ongoing attention to channeling, séances, and spiritualism. (Harry Houdini attempted to expose spiritualism as fraud years ago. It is not only still with us but it's bigger than ever.) In the midst of my doubts, though, I keep coming back to a dream I had. About a year before this dream, a man I'd tried to help killed himself. I didn't see it coming, so I blamed myself. Then I had this dream. I met this man and we sat down to talk. I expressed my sadness that I'd been unable to help him, and he spoke to me with a great deal of reassurance. Then he stood up and started to leave. I asked him where he was going and he turned and said, "Well, I'm supposed to wander for a while."

When I was younger, Catholics made a big deal about purgatory, a sort of waiting room of suffering from which you were eventually released and allowed into heaven, especially if people prayed for you. I still wonder if perhaps I had a glimpse into purgatory with this dream.

REFLECTION: What are your beliefs and questions about an afterlife? Have you had any experiences that gave you a glimpse of the afterlife?

Most who believe in an afterlife without any doubts are either taking a leap of faith or have had some sort of experience that they take as proof of an afterlife. But if indeed there is some theme of justice in the afterlife, we come back to the notion of sin. If there is an afterlife, does our conduct influence what we experience there?

The morality of the *Baltimore Catechism* was fairly black and white. We were told pretty clearly what actions sent us to hell. But I remember some more enlightened points of view that at the time were dismissed. I remember a nun in the third grade telling us it was a sin to have a toy gun. I remember another nun telling me that when I picked on a certain boy in class I was picking on Jesus Christ. At the time, those thoughts made no sense to me. Now they do.

The *Baltimore Catechism* had a certain appeal in that it seemed to make things clear as to what was and wasn't sinful. But events eventually called some of those core beliefs about sin into question.

Later on in school (I recall clearly when I was a freshman in high school), we used a teenage version of the *Baltimore Catechism* for religion class. Early on, Father JFP, SJ, called our attention to a section that listed the effects of "impure acts." They were horrifying! Brain damage! Insanity! (Interestingly, no mention was made of warts.) Father JFP then said, "Boys, you need to take all this with a grain of salt." This was unheard of (mind you, he was not saying that impure actions were OK). He was, in essence, giving us permission to question the *Baltimore Catechism*. It was also from the Jesuits that I first heard of an "informed conscience." The Catholic Church in fact taught that the primary source for determining right from wrong was my own conscience, informed by Church teaching and, even more so, by the guidance of Jesus.

Then came the Vietnam War and protests. I began to struggle with what appeared to be, on the one hand, a strong pacifist message from the Gospels. Yet on the other hand was the Catholic Church's position of "a justifiable war." Again I had to think about and decide what I believed (and still do, for that matter).

Finally, there was the issue of birth control. In the late 1960s, the Catholic Church and Pope Paul VI undertook a study of this issue. Although the majority of the advisory group recommended to the pope that he allow birth control, Paul took a minority position and outlawed it. Father BS, SJ (another Jesuit!), encouraged us to read both documents and to think. In the process, he pointed out to us that Catholic theology put primacy on the individual informed conscience. So again I chose to think about and decide what I believed. Such thinking and decision-making probably began to undermine the faith of my childhood! For a time, I felt guilt and fear about such erosion. I now think that perhaps the words of Fathers JFP and BS were turtles on fenceposts.

REFLECTION: Have you ever had to make an informed choice of conscience? Did that choice conflict in any way with teachings you'd received from formal religion?

The challenge here is to examine what you truly believe about right and wrong, to examine what you consider to be sinful and why. Once again, these can be frightening waters to tread along the Doubters' Way. There is security in having right and wrong drawn out for us by some authority figure. After all, the Ten Commandments do seem pretty clear. But in the absence of an overriding philosophy about right and wrong, such rules become merely guidelines.

When I look back at the faith of my childhood, I realize there was no overriding philosophy to guide my choice-making. I believe such a philosophy can be found in the words of Jesus. It can just get lost to rules and regulations. As noted in the listing of his unpopular sayings, he seemed to stress a few basic themes: loving ourselves and one another, nonviolence, nonattachment to possessions, humility. Where questions and doubts come in is how such a philosophy translates into daily ethical decisions. This depends upon your notion of what constitutes sin.

Being a Christian is somewhat of a popular thing nowadays and even seems to bear some political weight. American Christians are a political force courted by politicians. American Christians can even get television shows canceled. But if you pay close attention to the Gospels and especially to Jesus' unpopular sayings, you might become uneasy for, as Wendell Berry once noted, the extent that Christianity is fashionable (in the United States), is that: fashionable. Religion has "little to do with what Jesus actually taught" (*Blessed Are the Peacemakers: Christ's Teachings about Love, Compassion and Forgiveness*, Counterpoint Press: New York, 2005, p. 3). Again you might sense where doubting can get you into trouble.

If I begin to question why I believe certain actions are wrong, I might discover that the driving forces behind those decisions are guilt and fear. I might even conclude that something I judged as sinful at some other time I no longer view that way. Take missing Sunday Mass for example. When I grew up, such an omission was a grievous sin. As such, many Catholics attended Sunday Mass not because of some value about one's relationship with God but rather out of guilt and fear. Then all of a sudden attending Mass on Saturday evening was OK. It counted. This was confusing in the same way that some Catholics were confused when eating meat on Friday was no longer a sin. Consider two scenarios, two persons on Judgment Day, if you will. Person No. 1 struggled throughout his/her life trying to find and hold on to a relationship with God. He/she read, prayed, meditated. As part of his/her search, he/she would from time to time take a break from Catholicism and not attend Sunday Mass. Person No. 2 never missed Sunday Mass. He/she typically attended with a wandering mind, often dozing off during the sermon. He/she would think about what to have for breakfast, whether the Dallas Cowboys would win that day, etc. When he/she left Mass, it would be forgotten until next week. Which of these two persons do you think might be honored in heaven?

REFLECTION: How much is your moral world influenced by guilt and fear?

The problem with rule-bound thinking based on fear and guilt is that it eliminates choosing. Thomas Merton said, "A moral code does not suppress choice, but educates and forms liberty. But for some, morality is opposed to...*any choice* (Merton's emphasis) at all..." (*Conjectures of a Guilty Bystander*, Image: Garden City, NY, 1968, p. 29). So there is the possibility that a truly moral person is making moral choices on something other than fear or guilt.

If we pursue such a path, we may conclude that the moral thing to do may in fact be a course of action that at one time we were told was bad. Thus, person No. 1 above may have concluded that, to establish a spiritual path of integrity, he/she needed to stand back from the Church of his/her youth. This is what I call sinning bravely.

REFLECTION: Have you ever sinned bravely?

In part, too, we come full circle back to your image of God. Is the God of your understanding a rule enforcer? If so, then it becomes important that you clearly understand and abide by those rules. But suppose the God of your understanding is more than that. Suppose he/she calls you to think about moral decisions, to choose in a wise and informed manner. Then you may find yourself back along the Doubters' Way, questioning and doubting.

We come back also to your beliefs about Jesus Christ. How do you view his teachings? Did he really mean what he said? Weigh this question carefully, especially if you choose to call yourself Christian. Take seriously Wendell Berry's warning that taking the gospels seriously or assuming they say what they mean and mean what they say "is the beginning of troubles" (*op. cit.* p. 55).

The concept of sin can also be challenged by exposure to two seemingly unrelated, even antagonistic sources: recovery and psychology.

With programs of recovery, one must conduct a "moral inventory," a summation of one's pattern of sin. But the conclusions from that inventory are not a laundry list of sins but rather a clarification of what is referred to as "character defects." In other words, the focus isn't so much on individual acts as it is on patterns.

Similarly, psychology (specifically the psychology of Carl Jung) talks about a facet of our psyche known as "the Shadow." Connie Zweig and Jeremiah Abrams define the Shadow as containing "... undeveloped, unexpressed potentials of all kinds. It...represents those characteristics that the conscious personality does not wish to acknowledge and therefore neglects, forgets, and buries..." (Zweig, C. & J. Abrams, *Meeting the Shadow: the Hidden Power of the Dark Side of Human Nature*, Jeremy P. Tarcher: New York, 1991, p. xviii). The Shadow is represented in literature both in Robert Louis Stevenson's classic *Dr. Jekyll and Mr. Hyde* and in the character of Anakin Skywalker/Darth Vadar in the *Stars Wars* saga. The problem with the Shadow is that it does not stay tucked neatly away in our unconscious. It pops out, often at inopportune times and, if not faced, can wreak havoc in our personal relationships.

REFLECTION: If you want a glimpse of your own Shadow, make a list of qualities reflecting how you like people to see you. Then list the opposite of those qualities. That second list will give you a glimpse of your Shadow. For example, I like to be perceived as laid back and nonjudgmental. Therefore, my Shadow includes the qualities of demandingness and judgmental arrogance.

REFLECTION: What can you acknowledge about your own Shadow?

To put it simply, our Shadow contains much that we might judge as sinful. OK so far. But here's where the waters get muddy. Jungian theory encourages us not only to face our Shadows but to embrace them! The idea is that if I can accept what I find in my Shadow, I may uncover some resources I didn't know were there. Lead becomes gold.

This notion of facing the Shadow begins to sound somewhat like redemption. But not the kind of redemption where "sin" is eliminated. Rather it is the kind of redemption where sin is transformed. From this perspective, for me to deal with that which I judge to be sinful, I don't deal simply with behaviors and try to repress them. I face whatever lies beneath those behaviors. I try to accept that part of myself, ultimately transforming it into something more positive. My violence can help me become more able to speak out of righteous anger. My lust can be transformed into a capacity for intimacy and a celebration of my senses. But first I would have to face my violence and my lust in all their ugliness and selfishness. You can't get to the good stuff by acknowledging the field of manure then walking around it. You have to walk through the field. You're not really facing your Shadow unless you feel humbled.

The related notion of "character defects" calls our attention to personality patterns rather than to significant acts. Thus at one point, for example, I focused on the character defect of "bad temper" rather than numerous outbursts in traffic and elsewhere. It helps a little if one has an underlying value to inform one's conscience. The underlying value for Christians is supposed to be, "Love your neighbor as yourself."

Either or both of these concepts put sin in a somewhat different light and may even change the way you think about sin. Both concepts give me a stronger sense of the meaning of redemption.

In any case, if I begin to look for an underlying principle that supports my moral decisions, I may end up struggling with the absence of such a principle or I may begin to reevaluate my moral decisions based on such a principle. For example, suppose you decide that the moral foundation of your moral decision-making is indeed the powerful statement above. This might throw you into a turmoil regarding your beliefs about war.

There are other ways to look for this anchor for a moral life. Buddhism presents the Noble Eightfold Path, which challenges us—among other things—to attend to the way we use words, the way we earn a living, the way we focus our energy. Such an approach balances our Judeo-Christian tradition of Ten Commandments, which basically tell us what not to do. Thinking such as the Noble Eightfold Path suggests what to do to live a moral life.

REFLECTION: What would you say is the anchor of your own moral life?

If we extract from the teachings of Jesus a few underlying principles, they might be the following:

1. **Simplicity.** In her book *Gift From the Sea*, Anne Morrow Lindbergh observed that modern American life consists of a pattern of multiplicity wherein demands are made on our time and energy.

As she does, just make a list of the demands of an average week. Bills to pay. Home repairs to be done. Phone calls to be returned. Lunch dates to be arranged. Showing up for work. Washing clothes. Answering e-mail. For most of us, the list is extensive. Lindbergh gives a sobering warning about multiplicity: "It does not bring grace; it destroys the soul" (*Gift From the Sea*, Signet: New York, p. 26). To simplify our lives involves reexamining our patterns of consumerism and trying to function more out of need than of want. It also involves taking time alone.

2. **Solitude.** Having a capacity to be alone and quiet is an endangered species. Solitude never was easy. It can be downright uncomfortable because it involves a meeting with oneself and one's compulsions, one's "Dark Side." Nowadays it's become a whole lot easier to avoid being alone, thanks to cell phones and other electronic devices, etc. But if we lose the capacity to become quiet, we lose the opportunity to meet ourselves honestly in all our sinfulness and therefore to be redeemed.

3. **Nonviolence.** There seems to me to be no way around the fact that nonviolence is at the heart of the messages of most world religions. We are indeed called to turn the other cheek in Christian terms, to save all sentient beings in Buddhist terms. As with unconditional love, however, nonviolence may be an ideal goal rather than a concrete quality in our lives. I may no longer get into fistfights as I did in my youth, but I still am not beyond violent words and gestures, especially while driving to work! A nonviolent way of life goes far beyond an absence of physical violence.

4. **Grace.** The religion of my youth made the most of "being in a state of grace" and, obviously, "falling from a state of grace" so that, for me at least, my only understanding of grace was that it

was a relatively good feeling I had when I hadn't yet sinned. I think perhaps grace is much more than the mere absence of sin.

A good friend once suggested that grace was God sharing his/her power. Interesting notion, especially if we think about what God's power is. Obviously the notion is absurd if we think in terms of raising the dead or parting the Red Sea. But suppose God's power can be found in those ways in which we are gifted.

Here it becomes important to think of these terms in a broad manner. There are indeed gifts of physical beauty, of athletic prowess, of intellect. But there are also creative gifts. There are gifts of humor. Some people are gifted with a capacity for empathy and compassion. Others have a way with animals. It just might happen that one's experience of grace comes with expressing one's gifts.

In examining grace in one's life, we must also hold ourselves accountable regarding whether we are open to "costly grace" or are willing to settle for "cheap grace" (again using Bonhoeffer's terms). For me, cheap grace is that warm, fuzzy spiritual feeling from my childhood whereas costly grace is the sense of exhausted peacefulness I might find after a long struggle that leads to a redemption (something like recovering from an addiction or anxiety). Perhaps grace is also found when we face suffering in a certain manner and grow from it. And perhaps grace guides us toward turtles on fenceposts.

REFLECTION: What have been your own experiences of cheap and costly grace?

Take some time and reflect on your own foundation for what you believe as far as moral behavior is concerned. Doubts and questions may point you toward choosing out of more than just guilt or fear.

Chapter Four

"God save me from sober and serious saints!"

SAINT TERESA OF ÁVILA

One of the ironies of accepting the challenge of questioning and doubting on one's spiritual journey is that, if you believe you have more questions than answers, that's probably a sign you're doing well and actually getting somewhere. But it doesn't always feel that way. The absence of answers can be discouraging. How do you know if you are on the right track? How will you know when your question is answered or your doubts appeased? We can feel like we're doing nothing but wandering aimlessly in the desert. This chapter examines some resources that can be a source of renewal and encouragement, which can help make the uncertainty more tolerable. The sources to be examined are imagination, dialogue, a journal, a sense of humor, and insights derived from other religious traditions.

Imagination

Do you ever wonder what Jesus Christ or Buddha or Muhammad looked liked? How they're voices sounded? What they talked about when they weren't "preaching?" Or how about some of the famous teaching tales? Do you ever try to picture the powerful story of the Good Samaritan? Do you have a visual image of the prodigal son coming home? We are all blessed with the powerful gift of imagination—being able to picture things on the movie screen inside our heads. With imagination, we can leap tall buildings in a single bound. We can win the World Series. And with imagination we can enrich faith.

With the miracle of modern computers we can put ourselves into our own imaginative scenes, (for example, a historic scene at the White House where Forrest Gump was able to shake hands with the likes of John Kennedy and Richard Nixon). Our imagination can place us into the events and stories as we imagine them in Scriptures. I can derive spiritual benefit by imagining myself as a variety of characters in some of Jesus' stories.

Many persons in recovery programs find comfort picturing themselves as the prodigal son. But it can also be useful and humbling picturing oneself as the brother of the prodigal son. "Oh no! I would never be so petty!" Really? Have you never been jealous because someone you know received something you felt he didn't deserve, such as a promotion? Have you never both resented and secretly envied someone whom you felt "got away with it?" In my own case, seeing myself as the brother of the prodigal son reminds me that I haven't always been an easy brother to have, often passing judgment on my own brother as he struggled. Comedians such as Bill Cosby have enriched our understanding of Bible stories by putting a lighthearted spin to them as he did with his classic retelling of Noah and the Ark.

Sometimes with our imagination we can put a slightly different spin on traditional views of certain stories. For example, poor Martha has taken a bad rap for years as being a workaholic. Here she is busying herself while Mary sits and listens to Jesus. Martha even gets criticized by him. But suppose a few hours later Jesus rubs his stomach, looks around and says, "I'm getting kind of hungry. How about you folks?" There's nothing on the stove, however, and Martha kind of looks back at Jesus, shrugs her shoulders and says, "You told me to sit and listen." Some fundamentalists will obviously take offense at such a lighthearted approach. Too bad. Suppose all the stories he told, all the events are there for us to interact with, not to just passively listen to.

The more relevant question may not be, "What Would Jesus

Do?" but rather "What Would I Do?" If I were on a small fishing boat in the middle of the raging storm, you bet I'd be scared! And if Jesus were clearly the "go-to guy" when it came to quieting seas, you bet I'd wake him up! Not because I had such great faith but because I was terrified!

Imagination doesn't necessarily make doubts go away. But it allows a different way of interacting with that which cause us to struggle. Recalling chapter 1, for example, I doubt very much that God is either male or female. But my struggle with just who or what God is has been given a breath of fresh air by picturing a feminine God. To that effect, I had no grandmothers growing up. But I did have my Aunt Peg, who loved me unconditionally. As such, the God of my understanding makes terrific peanut butter cookies!

Finally, the use of imagination can be an interesting and enriching approach to prayer. Carl Jung developed the technique of active imagination to approach understanding our dreams, and John Sanford, Morton Kelsey, and others have expanded that technique to incorporate spiritual themes. Thus, one time I had a dream where I was in a prison. I imagined myself sitting there and pictured Jesus coming up outside the cell. In the image, I asked him, "Lord, help me get out of here." His answer that came to me was, "The door's unlocked." I stood up and pushed the door open and Jesus kind of chuckled. What I got from that was a reminder that any way I imprison myself, be it addiction, resentment, etc., is of my own making and the solution is easily available if I just turn to God. Helpful and humbling.

REFLECTION: Has your imagination enriched or assisted your travels on the Doubters' Way? If so, how?

Journal

One of the problems with doubts is that they can feel like mazes with no escape. We can be meditating or reading and have an insight that for the moment parts the clouds. But then the insight slips away. Or perhaps we just have no sense that we are getting anywhere in addressing our doubts. In these and many other areas, a journal can be of great help.

First of all, writing about your doubts in a journal gives form to the doubts, taking them out of the realm of vague anxieties. As they take form, you have a better sense of direction in terms of addressing them. If, for example, I write down, "I don't have a clear sense of just who or what God is," there can be some relief from simply naming the doubt. Then I have some sense of where I need to think or read. Such thinking or reading might be quite different from the thinking or reading I might do in response to the doubt, "I don't understand why bad things happen to good people and good things happen to bad people." Naming the doubt in a journal is a starting point.

Most doubts involve complex issues. Therefore it can also be helpful to keep a written record of the struggling process with a given doubt. For example, say I come across a thought of Viktor Frankl's that I find helpful. Perhaps a friend or client shares some of his/her own thoughts on the issue. By writing these down, I prevent them from slipping away in the midst of the fog of doubt.

In a similar vein, it can be an interesting exercise to have one sheet of paper and across the top of the page write "What I Know to Be True." Here you would write down not so much hard facts such as Dustin Pedroia's batting average but rather spiritual truths you have been able to determine hold for you. My list is not very long and certainly not profound, but I share it with you to give you a sense of developing your own list:

1. There is a God.
2. Learning to love ourselves and one another is the main reason we are here.
3. Grace is real.

That's it. Wish there was more. In any case, that brief list is nonetheless a comfort to me because I can read it and have a deeply felt sense of "Yes!"

REFLECTION: Create your own list of "What I know to Be True."

Your journal can also be a place to confront and express any anger you may have toward God. The simplest way to do this is to write God an angry letter. This may seem odd and, after doing so, you may for a moment fear being struck by a lightning bolt. But, given that God is not likely to show up for a personal confrontation in the way that he/she did with Job, writing a letter personalizes the feeling and therefore moves it closer to being resolved. Remember that anger left unexpressed tends to fester and to poison relationships, even a relationship with God.

REFLECTION: Write an angry letter to God. If you're not angry, then write to God about your doubts.

There are other uses for a journal, including dreamwork, prayer, venting about relationships, etc. As we will see in the next chapter, your journal can also be a safe place for you to go and be creative.

Companions

Phillip Simmons made an important observation about the spiritual path, noting that so much of our spiritual lives revolves around an interior journey. Yet, for most of us, "spirituality gets expressed—and often transformed—…in our relationships with others" (*Learning to Fall: The Blessings of an Imperfect Life*, Bantam: New York, 2002, p. 64).

Introverts are drawn to paths of reflection and interior wandering. These individuals can lose sight of the fact that part of the whole point of spiritual exploration is to improve the manner in which others are treated. The inward journey is mere narcissism unless we allow it to make us better lovers.

Beyond that, we can get caught up in the power of our realizations, risking becoming prideful. After all, Thomas Merton warned us that the most dangerous man is the one who is a contemplative but guided by nobody (*New Seeds of Contemplation*, New Directions: New York, 1961, p. 194). This doesn't necessarily mean that we must share our journeys with those who somehow know more about such journeys. There is, after all, no correct way to journey. Rather, it means that we must simply share our journeys. In this way, we receive another point of view, which is always helpful. And we test out in relationships all that we've come to know within.

The value of a companion is especially true when it comes to doubts and questions. As we talked about in the introduction, some of us may feel a little ashamed for having doubts. Sharing those doubts can break the back of such shame. A companion is not necessarily one who claims to have answers to our questions. A good companion is one who at least can affirm the question and can share his/her insights without any expectation that we must accept his/her answer. And most especially, a good companion does not judge.

As you seek out a suitable companion for your own journey, it really works best if the relationship is mutual, that is, if you also serve as companion for the other person's own journey. To be selected to serve as a companion on someone's spiritual journey must be viewed as a singular honor. In addition to the qualities mentioned above, if you are to serve as someone's spiritual companion, it is essential to develop a capacity to listen.

Can you recall a time when you felt really listened to? It is a rare and memorable experience. Listening is more than simply pointing your ears toward the sound of a person's voice. Listening is interactive. It involves requests for clarification. It involves the time-honored technique of reflection. ("What I'm hearing you say is....") It involves paying attention, a difficult accomplishment in this age of distraction. In that regard, I recall a gift given to me by my son, Ben. He came into my workroom where I was writing something and asked if he could talk to me. I turned halfway away from the computer so I could see my son but also have an eye to the computer. After a moment of this, Ben gently asked, "Dad, can I have your full attention?" Listening is a gift, just as much as having someone to listen.

REFLECTION: Do you have any companions along the Doubters' Way? Write about them. Have you expressed gratitude to them?

REFLECTION: Have you been a companion to anyone else walking along Doubters' Way? How has that affected you?

Spiritual Mentors

A mentor is a special type of companion. A mentor is someone who has followed a similar path as ours but is perhaps further along. A sponsor would be one example. Such mentors don't tell us what to do, but rather they share in the experience, give you strength, and generate a feeling of hope. Obviously in my case, I would relate best to a mentor who has struggled on the Doubters' Way.

REFLECTION: Have you had any personal mentors along the Doubters' Way. How have they helped you?

We might also find mentorship in someone else's writings. Thus, though I have never met any of them, I consider some of my spiritual mentors to be C.S.Lewis, Thomas Merton, Thich Nhat Hanh, Dietrich Bonhoeffer, and Henri Nouwen. Their sharing of their journeys through their writings have blessed my own struggling immensely. They have all been turtles on fenceposts for me: signs that my path, though filled with questions and doubts, is my own faith-filled path.

REFLECTION: Have you had any spiritual mentors such as writers, poets, playwrights, etc.? How have they helped you?

Other Traditions

One of my areas of great doubt has centered on the Catholic claim to being the One True Faith. For that matter, I have problems with the notion that Christianity of any sort is the only pathway. I find myself resonating to the words of Thich Nhat Hanh: "I do not see any reason to spend one's whole life tasting just one kind of fruit. We human beings can be nourished by the best values of many traditions" (*Living Buddha, Living Christ*, Riverhead: New

York, 1995, p. 2). And even more so do I respond to the words of Gandhi, who claimed that "religions are different roads converging to the same point." We take different roads; why should it matter "so long as we reach the same goal?" (*The Essential Gandhi*, L. Fischer, ed., Vintage: New York, 1983, p. 122).

Obviously if you don't struggle with doubts, you are unlikely to be interested in what different traditions have to say (as I will point out from my own experience shortly) and how they can enlighten your faith journey. But then again if you don't struggle with doubts, it's unlikely you've read this far.

As best I can recall, my introduction to Zen Buddhism came through Alan Watts' writings. I became curious about Buddhism through a speech given by the great family therapist Salvador Minuchin in which he compared the evolution of a family therapist to the training of a Samurai warrior. Eventually I would come to read a great deal about Buddhism and to be greatly moved by different writers, but particularly by Thich Nhat Hanh. What Buddhism brought to me was a deeper appreciation of the virtue of simplicity, a stronger commitment to nonviolence and, ironically, a deeper sense of the power of grace.

Being raised Catholic, I grew up with a certain bias against Judaism, a bias that fortunately I was eventually able to challenge and overcome. As such, I came to know *Jewish Literacy* by Joseph Telushkin. I came to know the writings of Abraham Joshua Heschel and of Lawrence Kushner. Through these thinkers and through dialogue with committed Jews open to dialogue, my own journey was enriched. I found fellow travelers struggling with the issue of suffering and willing to wrestle with God about such issues. I found a new appreciation for the Old Testament, something I tended to avoid, associating it with the fearsome God of my youth.

Through study of American Indian spirituality, I came to a deeper appreciation of nature as a manifestation of God's presence and a greater sense of the interconnectedness of all of creation.

I can promise you, however, that if you embrace the value of other traditions, you may come under criticism. So, again, be aware that pursuing the Doubters' Path may not endear you to some who espouse their own path with certainty.

REFLECTION: What has been your experience with different religious traditions? How have they affected your journey?

Sense of Humor and Fun

A final tool of immense value is to keep your sense of humor in your back pocket as you traverse these roads. There is a tendency in exploring spiritual matters to become very serious about the entire enterprise. We might end up taking ourselves entirely too seriously. When that happens, there is no fun to be found on the spiritual journey.

Fun? Do you find that to be a discordant word to find in the midst of exploring spiritual matters? Most of us do. And yet play seems so healthy, doesn't it? And laughter always seems to have a way of putting matters into a better perspective. Thus, two key qualities surface to nurture on the Doubters' Path, which are the capacity for fun and a healthy, self-effacing sense of humor.

Was Jesus Christ really such a serious dude? I hope not, but there is that tendency for him to be portrayed in that manner. Granted, being crucified was no walk in the park but, prior to that event, people did seem to be drawn to him and to enjoy his company. Do you like hanging out with people who are always serious and gloomy? The writers of the gospels seem to have missed capturing this side of Jesus (but if you've learned anything up to this point, your imagination can take you to the necessary level). How different the story would read if, in addition to "Jesus wept," we also were to read, "Jesus laughed."

So is there any sign of a lighthearted Jesus to be found? I think so. I mentioned earlier his encounter with children. The way the story reads is that children approached him. If you know children at all, then you know that children don't tend to approach adults who seem all serious and somber. They are drawn to adults who laugh and play. They see such adults as approachable.

I am not sure what Jesus meant when he urged us to become like children if we wish to enter the kingdom of heaven. But, in my imagination, I do see Jesus roughhousing with kids, letting them ride on his back as he got down on all fours and pretended to be a donkey. What if children were drawn to him not because he was the Son of God but because he was fun!? This allows me to apply my own life to my spiritual life. Some important people on the current part of my spiritual journey are my five grandchildren. They help me remember to have fun and to laugh.

REFLECTION: How does fun fit into your journey along the Doubters' Way? What do you consider to be fun? Are you able to play, especially with children? What makes you laugh? Who is your favorite comedian? Is it OK to laugh out loud in church?

These are important questions to address as part of the spiritual journey. Although things have gotten a little better, time was that the only thing that provoked laughter in the midst of Mass was if someone farted. Unfortunately, such laughter merited a few clicks from Sister's clicker if not a few swats from the yardstick. But we have this intriguing thought from Anne Lamott: "...Laughter is carbonated holiness" (*Plan B: Further Thoughts on Faith*, Riverhead: New York, 2005, p. 66).

I have often stated that a special place is reserved in heaven for comedians. Why? Because there is something very special about the capacity to make others laugh, and there is something life-giving when we do laugh, especially when we laugh at ourselves. That need to laugh at ourselves extends to how we view the spiritual journey. As Teresa of Ávila once warned, "God save me from sober and serious saints!"

Who or what makes you laugh? There have been some comedians who get me laughing as soon as they walk on stage, Jack Benny and Jonathan Winters being two in particular. There are movies that make me laugh even when I am watching them for the hundredth time. In discussing clowns, Ann and Barry Ulanov observed that clowns (as their example explains) poke holes in our universe. By doing so, a larger sun may shine through, visions of larger "things" can be glimpsed (*The Witch and the Clown: Two Archetypes of Human Sexuality*, Wilmette, Illinois: Chiron, 1987, p. 204). Thus, our comedians help us laugh at ourselves, keeping things in proportion, especially at a spiritual level.

REFLECTION: Where has humor showed up in your spiritual journey?

The issues confronted on a journey of questions and doubts are serious. But that seriousness in itself can be alluring. Viewing ourselves as weighed down with the profound issues is ultimately an ego trip. Even in the desert, I am just one more lost fool trying to find my way. Laughter reminds me of that.

Chapter Five

"Any path can become the Path if attended to with care, without preconceptions, and open to surprises."

CHET RAYMO

What has become clear to me as I struggle with doubt—much less write this book—is that the Doubters' Way is as much a way of life as it is an intellectual stance. Thus, embracing the Doubters' Way involves more than posing questions. It is to be lived in a certain way, and that way is summarized by the word integrity.

Integrity is a word we hear less and less. Sad. The Merriam-Webster dictionary gives us three meanings for integrity:

1. firm adherence to a code of especially moral or artistic values;
2. an unimpaired condition;
3. the quality or state of being complete or undivided

These definitions are a good starting point for you to understand the lifestyle you embrace should you try to follow the Doubters' Path.

The first definition makes it clear that becoming a Doubter does not mean that one becomes amoral. In fact, it's quite the opposite. To doubt and question means that I am demanding of myself the development of and adherence to a code of ethical behavior that I have thought about to the extent that I believe it to be true for me. It is a code of behavior I embrace because I have thought about it, not because someone else told me this is the way to act. Because I am a Doubter doesn't mean that somehow I am no longer a sinner. I am not excused from sin.

The second definition reflects the awareness that doubting is a way of life, a state of being. It's not that I go around all the time in a state of deep reflection. But being a Doubter does mean that I always remain open for light, for guidance and that I am open to such light and guidance coming from unexpected places. Some years back my philosopher-theologian son, Andy, when he was about ten years old, said to me, "Dad, if God is all-loving and loves all of creation, wouldn't he even love Satan?" That really made my head spin! I still think about that statement.

Even more to the point was a story I heard of a lady, dead drunk one night and watching a televangelist who was exhorting viewers to "lay your hand on the television set" to receive a healing. Now I had long rejected and even made fun of such histrionics. But this lady fell to the floor, crawled to her TV, put her hand on the TV, and passed out. The next day was her first day of what became long, rich sobriety.

The third definition reflects the awareness that, if I am going to walk the Doubters' Way with integrity, I can't pretend I'm something else. I can't present myself as a confirmed believer if it suits the situation. This doesn't mean that I reject Mass, for instance. It just means that, when I attend Mass, I show up with all my doubts.

I've realized that even doubt can have a dark side. I can become so certain of uncertainty that I acquire the same type of intellectual smugness which I reject in organized religion. In other words, in the midst of my questions, I can become arrogant. I can convince myself that I see inconsistencies or loopholes or something else that others don't see and am therefore more enlightened. I can ignore the guideline of theologian Hans Kung (another troublemaker) who made the point that "criticism of another position can be justified only on the basis of vigorous self-criticism" (*Theology for the Third Millennium: An Ecumenical View*, Doubleday: New York, 1988, p. 238). I'd like to propose to you the thought that walking the Doubters' Way with integrity involves the cultivation of four qualities or stances: honesty, humility, respect, and courage.

Honesty involves both speaking the truth and being open to the truth as I understand it. There is the obvious honesty of facing and accepting one's doubts. I can assure you that, as a lifelong Catholic, it is not easy for me to admit that, for example, I do not understand what "transubstantiation" means. Oh, I know what the word means, but the thought that somehow that bread and wine is the body and blood of Jesus? I don't get it. It's hard for me to understand, much less accept, which is not easy for me to admit. So if I am honest, I may come under attack by my own inner critic.

Similarly, while we Doubters may not go around advertising our doubts, we are called to speak our truth, which, too, can bring criticism to us. You may remember me suggesting reading the Twenty-third Psalm and substituting "she" for "he." I did this in speaking to a church group. One man stood up and accused me of being "a feminist" (which I actually took as a compliment, although it was not meant as one). I have also been called "a secularist," a "New Ager," and "an enemy of the Church."

Even more difficult is being open to the truth. This means, among other things, that I must develop a capacity for silence because most inner truths only come to us out of the storm of silence. Silence has become an endangered species in our culture. Silence has fallen victim to the onslaught of the cell phone and more technological forms of communication. Where once we might use a quiet moment on a bus or in our car to collect our thoughts, to pray, or perhaps to simply notice the sun setting, now we dial someone for no particular reason and fill those moments with noise. Why have we killed off silence? Perhaps it scares us. When we are quiet, we find out what we really think and feel. We find out what our hopes and dreams are. We face our failures and our shame. We remember lost loves. We run into grief we've been avoiding. Doris Grumbach speaks to some of the risks: "One must go into himself armed to the teeth...but also wearing a full plate of armor....Even so protected, one is still not safe from assault by the guerrilla forces of painful memories and deeply hidden guilt" (*Fifty Days of Solitude*, Beacon Press: Boston, 1994, p. 91). I might add doubts to her list of inner dangers. In any event, perhaps it's not too late. Perhaps we can still save the endangered species of silence.

REFLECTION: This coming week, try silence a time or two. Turn off the iPad. Don't automatically reach for the cell phone. Go for a walk in the desert. Be quiet and listen. You might find a doubt or even a poem inside you.

How is one dishonest with oneself? It's largely by avoiding or denying. I may come upon something uncomfortable and so will busy myself doing something else to distract me. Or perhaps I discredit an unsettling line of thought, saying something like, "Must have been something I ate." Keep in mind, too, that the one sure indicator of honesty is when I hear something I don't like.

REFLECTION: What experiences of honesty and dishonesty have you had along your spiritual journey?

When we think of humility, we often think of someone groveling or we may think in terms of self-criticism. Neither notion is correct. To be humble means to have a balanced view of oneself (in touch with the negative, yes, but also with the positive). Thus the humble person acknowledges those things about him/her that are sinful but also that which are saintly. If I focus only on the sin, then in some ways I am arrogant, touting myself as the World's Biggest Sinner, when in fact we are all a bit of both.

Doubts by their nature ought to be humbling. A doubt, after

all, is a state of not knowing. The humble person knows a few things (remember your list of "things I know for sure") but doesn't know even more. If you are doing well along the Doubters' Way, then you, too, should indeed rejoice if you figure something out or become enlightened in some way. But (being on the Doubters' path) it's just as important to remain aware of how much you don't know.

This quality of humility actually gets at the heart of what I am arguing here. The presence of, and awareness of, doubts does not make one "less than." Rather, the presence of (and struggling with) doubts may actually mean that I am on the "right path." Robert Ellsbery makes a similar point in his introduction to Brian Moore's wonderful novel *Catholics*: "...The tension between belief and doubt is not a contest between 'true Catholics' and the general mass of modernists. It is a tension that runs through the heart of every believer" (Loyola Press: Chicago, 2006, p. xii). The humble Doubter then is acutely aware of how much he/she does not know, how much he/she is struggling to believe. The humble Doubter does not broadcast his/her doubts as if they are profound and important insights. Nor does he/she scoff at others who appear more certain in their beliefs.

Finally, the humble person is able to acknowledge his/her gifts. Humility does not mean an absence of gifts. It simply means that I do not claim to be the originator of those gifts.

REFLECTION: What are your gifts?

Respect grows out of humility. It means that not only do I not think less of others who walk a different path but that I am open to the possibility that anyone I encounter may be a source of enlightenment or guidance for me. Doubters have been subjected to plenty of criticism. As a result, we should have a special sensitivity to its impact. Beyond that, when anyone shares his own point of view, the respectful Doubter accepts that the other person's walk may work for him/her and that perhaps something the other person has learned may be of help to me. In my own life, the clearest example of such persons for me have been persons of Simple Faith.

By Simple Faith I do not mean simplistic. The persons I've known who live a Simple Faith in fact have great depth to them. Their walk does not quite work for me, but I have learned much from them. Here's what I have learned from them:

Simple Faith holds love to be the supreme virtue and charity an important expression of that love.

God is in charge and there is a plan.

There is no room for passing judgment on others.

Simple Faith is hard work.

My mother was a person of Simple Faith. She strove to be loving and charitable. She dealt with a fair number of hardships throughout her entire life, such as her own mother's death when she was six years old and the deaths of my sisters, always with quiet resignation and acceptance. She never forced her brand of Catholicism down anyone's throat. And as she lay dying, saying she was "going home to see my girls," Saint Paul's words of 2 Timothy 4:7 in the *New Revised Standard Version* came home: "I have fought the good fight, I have finished the race, I have kept the faith." She made it to the finish line of a long, exhausting marathon.

There have been others. While all have their own unique hardships, they've all demonstrated the same strength and power in their Simple Faith. They never acted as if they had all the answers. Rather, they drew upon their faith quietly, and steadily, to cope with what life dished out. I envy them. And I certainly feel a higher sense of respect for them.

REFLECTION: Have you known persons of Simple Faith? How have they affected you as you struggle on the Doubters' Way?

The Doubter deals with himself/herself and others from a position of compassion. We Doubters are certainly compassionate with other Doubters. But we are also compassionate with those who have given up trying faith. We show compassion, too, for those caught in the trap of certainty and judgment. We show compassion for the arrogant ones because we know within ourselves our own potential for arrogance.

The Doubters' Path includes a call to courage. Remember that courage is not an absence of fear but rather not acting on that fear. Of what can Doubters be afraid? Rejection, judgment, and, most especially, being wrong.

The first two fears occur within the social domain. If I express my doubts in some honest manner, other believers may distance themselves from me, in part because of their belief that doubts are wrong. Still others may distance themselves because of not wanting to risk my planting seeds of doubt in their fields.

In a similar vein, if I express my doubts in any manner, I risk being judged as weak, sinful, etc. Remember that questioning some things may be perceived as a challenge.

You may also have seen that sometimes our doubts are about theological matters, but sometimes our doubts may have to do with a specific religion or the structure of that religion. For example, I have a huge doubt about Catholicism being the One True Faith. Among other things, when I look at the pedophilia scandals, when I consider my religion's response to the Holocaust, I tend to think, "If we're the One True Religion, we certainly have messed up and are in big trouble!" The expression of some doubts may involve questions about organized religion. Examples of questions I have posed also include, "Is celibacy necessary for the priesthood?" and, "How supportive of a meaningful role for women is my Church?" Such questions can obviously make you unpopular within the halls of power, much less your parish rectory. But one following the Doubters' Way persists in such questions, not so much to disrupt, but mainly to at least understand, to figure out what to believe.

The biggest fear plaguing Doubters, though, may be the fear of being wrong. Let me give you an example. Some time ago I was discussing anger with God with a very spiritual woman I've known for many years. Like me, she'd had a traditional Catholic education, one that discouraged anger with God. After I shared my point of view, she nodded, saying that made sense. Then she paused, looked at me with a twinkle in her eye and asked, "But suppose you're wrong?" The only thing I could think to say was, "Well then, I suppose when I go to board the bus to hell, there'll be a number of people waiting for me outside the bus with tire irons in their hands."

I wonder about such things. Suppose God really is a punisher. Suppose hell really exists and is the abode for those who doubt. Suppose Catholicism is the One True Faith to be accepted and lived without question. I don't know. What I think, though, is that perhaps we are called to follow a path honestly, to seek answers, to struggle, and especially to not let fear or complacency rule our spiritual paths. In other words, to walk with integrity.

REFLECTION: Take some time and evaluate how well you are walking the Doubters' Way with integrity. Is there room for improvement? (I hope so!)

Chapter Six

"The road to the sacred leads through the secular."

ABRAHAM JOSHUA HESCHEL

The Doubters' Way is not some detour. It winds right through the center of the city. It is not made up of some set of obscure questions such as, "How many angels fit on the head of a pin?" The Doubters' Way takes to heart the humanness of doubting. The concern is not in how we worship, whether we are doing it right or wrong. It's, rather, how we live and how we understand our lives. In other words, the Doubters' Way should carry us into life, not away from it. Beyond that, the Doubter maintains an open mind. As Anne Morrow Lindbergh wrote, "We must use any signposts that exist to help us through the wilderness" (*Gift From the Sea*, Signet: New York, 1955, p. 96).

We have already discussed several turtles on fenceposts. For me, most of my turtles have been people (I hope they are not offended). One thing I have learned is that, to identify someone as a turtle on a fencepost, I need to ask and to listen.

My job allows me to ask people how they function spiritually. Oddly, people tend to be private about their spiritual worlds (in part, I think, for fear of being exposed as a Doubter). If you begin to ask those around you, "Tell me about your spiritual world," you might be met with some hesitation. Don't let that deter you. Once others sense that you're not out to push a particular point of view, they may open up. So remember to listen.

Some long years ago, a woman came to consult. After she gave a brief introductory explanation of why she'd come, I launched into a diatribe about what she needed to do. She listened politely, then put up her hand and said, "Would you just listen?"

As a Doubter learning to listen, you might hear something important. You might hear someone share a struggle of her own and how she coped. You might simply be reassured that you are not alone in your struggles. Similarly, as you listen to some people talk about how they draw upon faith to face tragedy, you may be humbled (as I was when the man I mentioned earlier who faced Lou Gehrig's disease spoke softly about how his faith gave him the strength to accept a terrible burden and that the God of his understanding would be there for his family when he was gone).

There are also a few collections of people's reflections on their spiritual journeys. I am not talking about the writings of saints. I am talking about works by the likes of Studs Terkel and Phillip Berman, writers who interviewed everyday people, saints in their own way but people nonetheless like you and me. Consider some thoughts from Ted Hayes, a homeless man interviewed by Berman. The homeless man emphasized to Berman that our highest goals and beliefs (that is, in God) must be "able to walk on earth," they need to be real (flesh), touchable. No matter what our faith—Muslim, Christian, Buddhist—if our God cannot "walk the earth," it means that we are not being the Muslim, Christian, or Buddhist we were called to be. Jesus lived on the streets with the poorest of the poor, and so should we (*The Search for Meaning*, Ballantine: New York, 1990, p. 148). Quite a teacher!

There are, of course, many spiritual autobiographies portraying the spiritual journeys of great people. Not just saints but artists, writers, philosophers. Some of these are hard going and ponderous. To find a starting point, you might look into an anthology such as *Pilgrim Souls: A Collection of Spiritual Autobiography*, edited by Amy Mandeleker and Elizabeth Powers (Touchstone: New York, 1999). This book includes excerpts from the writings of spiritual voyagers like Saint Augustine, John Wesley, Eldridge Cleaver, Annie Dillard, and Flannery O'Connor. Some unconventional spiritual autobiographies that I have found helpful include Rick

Bragg's *All Over But the Shoutin'* (Random House: New York, 1997), Pope John Paul I's *Illustrissimi* (Little, Brown, and Co.: New York, 1978), and *All the Strange Hours* by Loren Eiseley (Charles Scribner: New York, 1975).

Each of us has a spiritual story worth telling. I hope you can create your own story, and as you develop your own list of spiritual autobiographies that you can relate to, I hope they will help sustain you on your own journey on the Doubters' Way.

REFLECTION: Are there any spiritual autobiographies that have helped you along the Doubters' Way?

To remain present in the real world, we also must remain open to the spiritual challenges presented to us by events, whether of a personal nature or more global. For example, 9/11 changed many people spiritually. Where was God in the rubble of the Twin Towers and the Pentagon or in the wreckage of Flight 93 in a Pennsylvania field? Some found a deeper connection. Others lost the one they had. More recently, some soldiers have found God in Afghanistan or Iraq. Others lost him or her in the midst of trials and tribulations.

Are there ways to measure whether we are making any progress, especially since the Doubters' Way is filled with paradox (in short, the more you are struggling, the closer you are to God)? Obviously we Doubters don't measure progress by close adherence to a specific set of beliefs. Quite the opposite.

Jerry Dollard (*Toward Spirituality: The Inner Journey*, Hazelden: Center City, MN, 1983) offers one possible road map that is not dependent on a specific set of beliefs. He suggests that spiritual progress can be measured along four movements: 1. from fear to trust; 2. from self-pity to gratitude; 3. from resentment to acceptance; 4. from dishonesty to honesty. You might sense some overlap with our discussion of integrity. Let's examine these movements further as they relate to the Doubters' Way.

In facing doubts, I am choosing not to act on fear. My fears say, "There are no answers. Nothing makes sense," or, "You will burn in hell if you doubt." If I examine a doubt, I am trusting that sense can be made of it and that I will not be punished. I am trusting that I am doing the correct and necessary thing by questioning. In other words, I trust that in facing my doubts I am acting morally.

This gets at the heart of one of my ancient fears—that somehow doubting is sinful. Can I prove that doubting is not a sin? No. Do I trust that not only is it not a sin but for some a virtue? A resounding YES!

REFLECTION: Is there anything about doubting that causes you fear?

Regarding the second movement, from self-pity to gratitude, we saw earlier that gratitude can be a tricky matter for Doubters. Self-pity is within easy reach. I can feel sorry for myself that I don't have answers. I can feel sorry for myself that others don't understand or accept my doubts; they perhaps even judge me.

To argue that one should be grateful for the capacity to doubt can get one into hot water in certain circles. Yet that is exactly what I am proposing—that you embrace your doubts with gratitude. The fact that you doubt means you are thinking and are not afraid to think outside the box. This is what all the great religious leaders invited others to do: think outside the box. Take Jesus for example. He suggested that what mattered was not how well you adhered to rules and regulations but rather how well you love. At that time, this was a radical notion and, in many ways, it still is.

I can also be grateful for my doubts because they are a sign that I will not simply accept some notion because someone in authority tells me I'm supposed to. Socrates once said that the unexamined life is not worth living. This may also apply to the unexamined faith—that it is not worth practicing. My doubts demand that I examine my faith, such as it is. For that I can be grateful.

REFLECTION: How do you feel about being a Doubter? Is there anything about doubting for which you can be grateful?

The movement from resentment to acceptance occurs both in our relationships with others and in our relationship with ourselves. Remember that Simple Faith includes an absence of judgment on another's progress in his relationship to faith. The same applies to the Doubter. We who doubt need to grow so that we do not resent those who espouse certainty.

We also need to resolve resentment toward those who have judged us. Throughout this work, I have touched lightly on judgment others have passed on me. The entire truth is that I have struggled with resentment toward these persons—the man who called me a feminist, the Church official who pronounced me an enemy of the Church, and others. I did not let these judgments roll off of me. They stuck and bothered me. But resentments of any sort are toxic, a spiritual cancer. It is dangerous to ignore them, lest they fester and poison our spiritual world. To accept this doesn't mean to condone it. It is simply to accept that, in walking the Doubters' Way, I will run afoul of some believers. Additionally, I need not resent myself. Vestiges of old tapes about doubts may give rise to my own judgment of myself as weak and sinful. I may find myself saying things like, "What's wrong with me? How come I can't/won't believe with the faith that so-and-so has? God must be disgusted with me." Such self-condemnation is a roadblock stifling our spiritual growth. We must accept that, for whatever reason, our path is one of questions and doubts.

REFLECTION: Do you hold any resentments toward others who have hurt you spiritually? Are you accepting of being a Doubter?

The final movement, from dishonesty to honesty, was addressed in the last chapter. Both qualities have a public and a private dimension. I can present myself to the public as something other than who I am. I can pose as a committed Christian, Jew, Buddhist, etc. I can act in public as if I fully embrace everything about a faith tradition. Or I can simply attend religious services if I so choose but do so humbly and quietly.

In the same way, I have to be brutally honest with myself that I even have doubts. Then I have to honestly confront those doubts. A painful and frightening process.

The successful Doubter, then, is one who is trusting, grateful, accepting, and honest. Your own self-assessment along those dimensions may give you a sense of how you are progressing along the Doubters' Way.

Chapter Seven

"Hope is a good thing, maybe the best of things.
And no good thing ever dies."

TIM ROBBINS AS ANDY DUFRESNE IN *THE SHAWSHANK REDEMPTION*

The premise of this work has been that, if you face and embrace your doubts, you may actually find faith. Beyond that, there are three other treasures that you may uncover along the Doubters' Way: creativity, an appreciation for the mystical, and hope.

I discussed in chapter one a view of God involved in ongoing creation and the invitation, (perhaps even the obligation) to participate in and further that creation. Nothing tends to stunt creation more than rules and rigid thinking. But when we begin to try to look at something from multiple angles or at least to entertain the question, "Is this the only way to look at this issue?" interesting things happen.

One of the things I loved about comedian Jonathan Winters was his improvisational ability to pick up a common object and transform it into something else. Thus, a pencil would become an oar, a blow-dart, a miniature dirigible, and so on, all coming from the thought of looking at that object differently.

And so when we open ourselves to looking at God from different angles or perspectives, when we approach the notion of sin from different roadways, we may begin to experience the opening up of creative energy.

Within the field of psychology, there is the notion that everyone has three "wills": the will to pleasure, the will to power, and the will to meaning. These "wills" have represented different theories about what is the central motivator of human behavior. Freud, with his theories of the unconscious and instincts, believed that we are ultimately pleasure-seeking creatures motivated to make decisions in terms of either pleasure or the avoidance of pain. Alfred Adler believed we were more driven by the desire for power and control. Viktor Frankl believed we are essentially creatures who must find meaning in our lives and so will make decisions based on what supports that sense of meaning and will become frustrated and depressed if that will to meaning is thwarted.

It occurs to me that there may also be an inherent need to create, a "will to create." If Teilhard de Chardin and others are right—that God indeed not only invites but expects us to participate in creation—then it would make sense that we are in some way "hard-wired" to be creative. This creative drive may manifest itself in traditional works of art but may also be expressed in other less obvious ways.

Most of us, when we think of creativity, tend to limit ourselves because we are not Van Goghs or Tennessee Williamses or Ben Kingsleys. We equate creativity with well-known artists. So, for a moment, I want you to join me in a little side trip in the desert. I want you to write a poem.

I've done the following exercise many times and remain amazed by the poetry inside each and every one of us. One of the things we all tend to like about poetry is the play with sounds, whether it is rhymes ("The cat sat on the mat") or recurring letters (for example, "I caught this morning morning's minion," by G.M. Hopkins). So the first step is to play with sounds and words. Pick a sound you like, say, "m." Play with it like so: Mmmmmm. My mud. My mucky mud. Or big Buddy's bowling ball. Enjoy playing with sounds and words.

Then consider a potent experience you've had. Jot down images of that experience, perhaps playing with sounds and words in the process. Here's an example, drawn from my several summers at a summer camp for children with cancer:

Young men and women
Cooling their rage with laughter.
An errant skunk.
Missing limbs and haunting beauty.
Loneliness here and there
In the eyes of campfire watchers.
Thunder at 3 PM.
Sunrises—a glimpse of God's smile
On little ones wise beyond their years.
A sadness in places as word passes
That someone didn't make it.
Hope—joyful, shouting, prank-filled hope
Given as a gift
By young teachers
To one who has so much to learn.

I also have this notion that sometimes a particular image stays with us, sometimes for years, because it is a poem waiting to come out. Such an image occurred for me in a poolroom in the basement of a nursing home:

So now you know.
This is where we old coal miners come.
Maloney Home.

Oh, it's not so bad.
The sisters....They feed us well.
Nurse us when we're sick.
Bury us when it's time.

But here's the joke.
Somewhere in the bowels of this building
A boiler room works day and night
To keep us warm.

That boiler runs on coal.
But they won't let me go down there.
I who know so much about those black rocks.
They won't let me go down there anymore.
They say I might get hurt.
That's the joke.

Finally we may find a poem in a moment of wonder when ordinary language falls short in capturing the power of that wonder. Such a moment for me is the culmination of the 1960 World Series:

Fall.
Burning leaves.
Light jackets.
The Series.

My Braves left long behind.
The vaguely known Pirates
Squeezing the hated Yankees
Into a seventh game.

Fall.

Red, yellow, orange leaves
Littered everywhere.
Scraped into piles for jumping.
But not today.
Pirates behind.

An errant ball, a misplaced pebble.
(Forgive me, Tony.
I cheered as you clutched
Your damaged throat.)

Walking home.

Radio pressed to a not-yet chilled ear.
Hal Smith (do I have his card?)
Now I run, in time for the 8th and 9th.

Long shadows.
Chipmunks scurry.
It's Maz's hour.
He swings
And Yogi watches
Like a little boy
Who let go of his balloon.

Nighttime.
Do I hear geese?
Do they know
What happened today?

REFLECTION: Think of an image from your past, a memory perhaps, or a moment of wonder. Write a poem and, even better, read that poem to someone for poetry is meant to be read aloud. You might surprise yourself.

There are so many ways to be creative above and beyond creating a work of art. Some people can cook things or uses spices. Others can grow things. Some parents are able to be wonderfully playful with their children. Some, when it comes to problem-solving, have a flair for "thinking outside the box." Creativity does not require intelligence, especially as traditionally understood. Sometimes a childlike mind can see things in a new, refreshing way.

The Doubters' Way can nurture our creativity. Doubts, after all, challenge a traditional accepted view of some theme. To doubt is the first step toward a creative solution. "Do I have to see God as a man? What happens if I let go of that limitation?" The door to creativity swings open!

Yet too often we step in and slam the door shut. Why? Two reasons, I think. One is our old friend "should." I should do something more productive, more useful. I should not waste my time on something trivial like writing a poem or performing in a play. But an even greater impediment to our creativity is fear. To create and, even more so, to share one's creativity is a great feeling of vulnerability. We can be subjected to criticism. (I still recall getting a "C" for a lopsided pumpkin I drew for Halloween.) Whenever I have done the above-mentioned poetry exercise, I always invite participants to share their poems aloud. There is always initial hesitation. That fear again. Thankfully, the desire to share the fruits of creativity eventually overrides the fear such that, often, I have had to end the sharing with some still wanting to share.

We fear criticism or, more deeply, rejection. With each book I've written I've had the same experience the day the first box of books arrives. I open the box anxious to see how it turned out. But then I have a moment of panic as I realize that my thoughts and words are no longer under my control. I am now vulnerable.

A related fear is that somehow what we create is of no value. How often I have heard people (including myself) say such things as, "I don't know how to draw," or, "I can't carry a tune," or, "I could never write a poem." How often I have written a piece then tossed it, thinking, "what a piece of junk. Worthless!" We are not all Pavarottis, but we can let a fear about the value of what we create become a block to anything creative.

Again the Doubters' Way helps here because, as we often noted, to walk this path involves tolerating a certain level of fear while still walking. It involves accepting a level of vulnerability, especially when one chooses to share one's doubts. As such, we acquire a certain familiarity with not allowing fear to make decisions for us.

The journal is a good place to explore your creative side, whether by writing poems, sketching, or just plain imagining. It is also a place to explore your fears of creating.

REFLECTION: In what ways are you creative? What do you do to nurture that creativity? Has fear limited your creative explorations?

As you walk the Doubters' Way, you may begin to sense the inadequacy of words when it comes to trying to capture something like "God" or even your thoughts and emotions. This is because, as we look more deeply and begin to look beyond what we are told to believe, we touch on what Jung called "the numinous," what my mother-in-law called "ineffable," or what may simply be called "the mystical." Rabbi Heschel said (rather succinctly) that to become aware of the indescribable is to move beyond trying to express it with words (S.H. Dresner, ed., *I Asked for Wonder; a Spiritual Anthology of Abraham*, Joshua Heschel, Crossroad: NY, 1990, p. 2).

When we hear the word "mystic" we tend to think of saintly people like Mother Teresa or Saint John of the Cross and despair of ever having a mystical experience. Yet I believe mystical experience is well within our reach. There is first of all the experience of wonder. Have you ever experienced something and struggled to find words that could adequately capture your experience? I can think of when I first laid eyes on each of my newborn children and grandchildren. I can think of an encounter with a herd of deer. I can think of being present at someone's death. These and other experiences had a profound effect upon me, yet I am hard-pressed to find words adequate to describe them.

We also touch on the mystical domain when we sense a deep connection with someone. Perhaps such deep connection is sensed through lovemaking. Perhaps it is sensed after a deep and open conversation. Perhaps it is sensed through a profound shared experience. I recall for instance standing with my wife at the JFK Museum in Dallas and looking down on Dealey Plaza and the sight of his assassination. I felt a connection beyond words with my wife in that moment of deeply felt sadness.

Surprisingly, because we doubt, we may be more open to manifestations of God found in unsuspected places, an observation suggested by David Wolpe's notion of the "normal mystic" as one who "looks at life as you and I know it, but with an acute eye, one that tracks the almost imperceptible or often overlooked suggestion of God in every corner, at each turn" (*The Healer of Shattered Hearts: A Jewish View of God*, Penguin: New York, 1990, p. 81).

Ironic, isn't it? We Doubters may detect God in ways believers miss. How can this be? Well, if I believe, for example, that I can only encounter God in a church, mosque, or synagogue, then I shall miss the glory of God in an El Paso sunset. I shall miss his/her voice in my grandchild's laughter. I shall miss God's tears at the 9/11 Memorial. Because we Doubters cannot be confined in where we search for God, there is a chance we will encounter God in surprising ways.

This for me is a great gift of the Doubters' Way.

REFLECTION: What have been your experiences of wonder or deep connection?

Perhaps because of its religious overtones, the word "hope" does not show up often in earlier psychological literature. A noteworthy exception was Jerome Frank. Frank's book *Persuasion and Healing* is something that should be read by anyone involved in the relief of human suffering. In articulating the factors that contribute to successful therapy, Frank describes five themes, all of which might be considered facets of a psychological view of hope. They are (summarized):

1. Addressing the patient's sense of alienation and finding strength. Hope is certainly impacted by a sense of belonging and by a sense that at least one another person cares enough to be willing to sit with us amidst the suffering. This reinforces the importance of sharing one's journey as a way of sustaining oneself.

2. Inspiring and living up to the expectation of helping the patient. As Frank notes, this expectation must be rooted in something tangible and realistic. In other words, hope must have an element of realism to it if it will have an impact on therapy.

3. Provide opportunities for growing/learning. Part of that element of realism relates to the possibility that change can occur. In other words, knowledge is power, and such power can be the vehicle of change. The Doubters' Way can lead into hopelessness if I do not sense some point to it, some meaningful change in my life such as an enriched faith.

4. Arousing emotion. It is emotion that can provide the force for powerful change. As Frank notes, emotional experience needs to be examined and integrated at the cognitive level, but it still provides movement. Religious revivalists have known this for years. So have AAers. (The experience of "hitting bottom," a key to recovery, is largely emotional in nature.)

Doubters may have developed a certain skepticism over emotionally tinged religious experiences. We discussed earlier retreat experiences where much emotion is aroused but little change actually occurs. On the other hand, dramatic changes in lifestyle do occur. Some would call them redemptive experiences. Emotion is typically involved. As such, those wandering the Desert of Doubt need not be leery of emotional experience. Rather they should be welcomed (but then examined).

Keep in mind, too, that a redemptive experience does not necessarily involve religion. Many addicts I have known were rescued from the pit without ever entering a church. The redemptive experience involves rising up out of total brokenness. It is probably the strongest experience we can have of hope.

REFLECTION: Have you had any sort of redemptive experience?

5. Enhance the patient's sense of effectiveness. Although some therapists might disagree, I believe we do people a disservice if we lead them to believe that any change that occurs is because of the power of the therapist, not because of newfound power within the client. It should come as no surprise to you by now that I also believe the same to be true about religion. My kingdom of God is within me, not within some priest, minister, or rabbi. I need to become clear that, just as Eric Liddell says in *Chariots of Fire*, the power comes from within. Otherwise I will be forever dependent on someone else for my own spiritual growth.

More recently, Charles R. Snyder has researched the topic of hope and has come up with a less involved definition. He views hope to be the combination of willpower and way-power that you have for your goals (*The Psychology of Hope*, Simon and Schuster: New York, 1994, p. 4). In other words, hope is a combination of commitment to a specific goal (willpower) as well as having the available means to accomplish that goal (way-power). If, for example, I wish to become a professional baseball player then, according to Snyder, I would need to have both the ability necessary for such a level as well as the willingness to dedicate time for practice. Snyder views hope from a very goal-oriented perspective and clearly grounds hope in a realistic appraisal of skill and self-discipline.

Snyder's research outlines what I believe to be a type of pragmatic hope. Such hope can sustain the Doubter by keeping a given goal in mind (a strong faith) as well as keeping the Doubter focused on persistent searching. However, I believe there is a different type of hope that is also relevant to the Doubters' Way: That is to hope in the unlikely and in the unseen.

Is it wrong for a person dying of cancer to have hope of a cure? Is it foolish to hope for a miracle? Some people would seem to believe that either one accepts the reality of one's situation or one has hope. Why aren't both points of view possible? Can one not prepare oneself to die while at the same time holding a hope for something unexpected?

Buddhism has a bit of problem with the concept of hope since hope tends to pull us into the future, away from the Buddhist emphasis on focusing on the present moment. Thich Nhat Hanh's caution is well-taken that, when we consider the nature of hope, it seems tragic. Since we cling to our hope as an outlook to the future, we do not focus our energies and capabilities on the present moment.

Equally slippery, however, is the concept of "the present moment." I remember when he was young, my son, Andy, asked me, "Dad, is it now everywhere?" An amazing question from a six-year-old! The present moment, the now, is even a part of the past as I focus on it. Much like a flowing stream. A film called *Off the Map* poetically captures my own sense of "the present moment": "It has struck me to view the ocean as the past, the sky as the future and the present as that precarious line where both meet; precarious because, as we stand there, it curves underfoot, ever changing." So we Doubters end up having questions and doubts about even something so basic as "the present moment."

REFLECTION: What are your experiences of hope? Where does hope fit in your spiritual journey?

Hope is indeed a good thing. There is much that I don't know, most of which I expect I'll never know. My faith is constantly changing and often seems lacking. Somehow I find the idea of hope sustaining. But hope for what? Let us conclude with some words of hope, a variation on the words spoken by Morgan Freeman at the conclusion of *The Shawshank Redemption*:

I hope there is a loving God.
I hope there is an afterlife and a heaven.
I hope to see my parents there and to meet my sisters.
I hope....

Conclusion

If you have stayed with me to this point, then you might fall into one of three categories.

You might be viewing my faith as weak and me to be misguided. If so, I invite you to recall Anne Lamott's observation that the opposite of faith is not doubt but certainty. You might also want to sit for a while with Jesus' caution that we don't judge lest we be judged.

You might be feeling sorry for me or be worried for me. If so, you are likely a person of Simple Faith. I envy you. Please pray for me.

You might also be a fellow Doubter. If so, I encourage you to embrace your doubts and to nurture them. The path we share requires courage.

I have been blessed with turtles on fenceposts. Teachers inviting me to think. Persons of courage facing terminal illness. Grandchildren.

I have seen miracles. I have even experienced a miracle as has anyone redeemed from addiction. Yet I still long for a neon sign that says "I exist!" I long for a parting Red Sea. Tumbling walls of Jericho. A Lazarus rising from the dead. I'd even settle for a talking donkey.

In that spirit, I leave you with words from a fellow Doubter, a soldier seeking Jesus' help: "I do believe, Lord, help my unbelief." Amen to that.

Appendix

Included here are some excerpts from my previous book *Writing Your Spiritual Autobiography*. I want to encourage you to develop your own spiritual autobiography as a tool to help you navigate the Doubters' Way. These excerpts can hopefully give you a sense of journaling and will serve as your first steps to writing your own story of spiritual travel. Enjoy!

Suffering

I am convinced that while my mother carried me she stormed heaven with prayer. She was frightened. My older sister had been born with spina bifida and died after three days. In those days, there was no way of knowing what was coming when you were pregnant. No ultrasound. No amniocentesis. You just prayed that whatever came out would have the right parts in the right places. My older sister didn't. As such, when my mother carried me, she had no idea what to expect.

Well, I turned out OK, more or less. I like to think I was a source of relief to my mother when I popped out with everything in the right place. But during my second year, my mother was again pregnant. There is a picture of me with my mother during this time. I have just plucked a pear from my grandfather's tree and am looking at my mother, who is smiling back. But she is pregnant and there is a bit of anxiety in her eyes.

My younger sister Linda was born about two months before my third birthday. She, too, had spina bifida. She lived four months, spending her last days in St. Joseph's Hospital.

We lived up the street from St. Joseph's Hospital, a truly mysterious place. It was a hospital first of all for unwed mothers, young women who were at times the subject of "fires of hell" sermons at the nearby Catholic women's college. It was also a home for children who were retarded or worse and could not live at home or did not have a home. We'd often see many of these kids outside playing. Inside there was a ward for those children who could not play—the ones with hydrocephalus and other horrifying deformities. In high school once as a social service project we toured St. Joseph's. When we came to that ward, one young man had to leave so he could throw up.

So St. Joseph's was a final stop for my sister and others of what? God's mistakes? My sister spent her final days in that ward and then, to quote my mother, became an angel.

Spina bifida is a congenital disease in which the spinal column does not fully close. Hydrocephalus can be one of the results. Nowadays children can survive, albeit with significant impairment. It is not a disease you get from smoking too many cigarettes or eating too much chocolate. You are born with it. No choice. No chance to undo the damage.

And so my two sisters set the stage for what would become a central struggle of my Catholic faith. What's the deal, God? What gives here? Not one but two kids born with a horrible deformity that killed them both? Did some Patterson somewhere offend you or what?

REFLECTION: In general, what kinds of suffering have you encountered which have not made sense to you?

The lives and deaths of my sisters were, of course, never discussed. I say "of course" because we were after all quite Irish Catholic and so adopted the standard ethnic position of silence. In fact, I learned of their existence only after paging through the family Bible one day after I'd learned to read. These were the days when family Bibles were also the holders of family records. And so on one page that listed significant births were the names Linda and Patricia. Patricia was listed as being born on December 12, 1946, and dying December 15, 1946. Linda was listed as being born in December of 1951, followed by the words in my mother's handwriting "Died in April." So it goes. This was where I first found these two girls who would have such a profound effect on my spiritual journey. My mother would answer questions I had. My father never spoke about them. And I spent many years wondering. What happened to them? What would life have been like if they had lived? And most especially, at some level even when I was young, why did this happen?

Whether my father believed that what happened to my sisters was a punishment for his sins, I do not know. My mother never questioned it. Life was made up of crosses to bear, she believed. You picked yours up and didn't argue. Neither my father's nor my mother's position ever worked for me.

In subsequent years, I was dogged by the "why" question. Not just about my sisters but about any suffering that seemed senseless. Why did this very good family lose a child to Reye's syndrome? Why do children die at all, much less of horrible, disfiguring diseases such as cancer? I have heard this preached about many times, the ultimate answer being, "It's a mystery." A Mys-ter-y. A Mys-ter-y. That answer over time began to sound like something out of a Gilbert and Sullivan operetta.

Sometime in 1988 I had a dream about my younger sister. I dreamed of her as a healthy adult. Like me, she was tall and thin. In the dream, she had a drinking problem and I was taking her for help. I took her to the door of the treatment center, then let her walk through. It was as vivid a dream as I've ever had, the kind where you wake up believing it to have happened. In that split instant between sleep and waking I thought, "A mistake has been made. She's alive. My sister's alive. She's out there somewhere." Then wakefulness took charge and I realized it was a dream. Some weeks later my wife mentioned my dream to my mother. This opened up the reality of my sisters for acknowledgment, so that when my mother was ready to die, she said. "My bags are packed and I'm going to see my girls."

C.S. Lewis wrote that Christianity creates the problem of pain, for pain would be no problem unless, side by side with our daily experience in the painful world, we had also a good assurance that ultimate reality is loving (see *The Problem of Pain*, Macmillan: New York, 1962, p. 24). By this he meant that, once we posit the existence of a loving God, then we are put in a position of trying to explain senseless suffering. No loving God? Then senseless suffering doesn't have to make sense. In a Godless world, ugliness and pain happen.

But this is not what I was taught. I was taught that God loves us. (Mostly. Actually, my early exposure to God was a bit more of a mixed bag. God both loves and punishes.)

Jewish people, too, have been challenged to make sense of suffering. The question "Where was God in the death camps?" has not only troubled many Jews but others as well. Where was God in the death camps? And if and when God does show up, what is it that we expect him/her to do about the suffering? Do we expect a miracle or do we content ourselves with God's compassion; that God isn't there to take away our suffering or our pain but, rather, to fill it with his or her presence?

Many of us, Jews and Christians alike, take comfort in the notion that the scales are balanced in the next life. Jewish belief is such that not only are we rewarded, but also the guys who did us dirty eventually pay up. We make sense of our suffering by putting a theological twist to the modern myth, "What goes around comes around."

I remember, though, a story told by Abraham Twerski (*Generation to Generation: Personal Reflections of a Chassidic Legacy*, Traditional Press: Brooklyn, 1985, p. 13). In the story, he describes a man in a prison. This man's job was to turn a wheel embedded in a wall. This is all he did for years. He dealt with this task by convincing himself that on the other side of the wall was a great and important machine that his turning helped to operate. Many of us deal with suffering in the same way. We believe that it makes some sense in the larger scheme of things. Indeed, the great psychiatrist Victor Frankl stated that this quality is one facet of being human. There is much suffering about which we can do nothing. But we can make some decision as to how we face such suffering.

Frankl wrote that man is not free from conditions, but he is and always remains free to take a stand toward these conditions (see "The philosophical foundations of logotherapy" in *Psychotherapy and Existentialism*, Simon and Schuster: New York, 1967, p. 3).

REFLECTION: What different stances have you taken toward suffering? What stances of others have you especially admired?

Frankl helps me make sense of what we can do in the face of suffering. But I am still left with the question of how such suffering adds up, and I am bothered by the nagging doubt that on the other side of the wall is—nothing!

I have read C.S. Lewis. I have read Annie Dillard. I have read Zen Buddhists. Anyone who offers the hope of some insight. Early on, I read Harold Kushner's wonderful *When Bad Things Happen to Good People*, (Avon: New York, 1997). Rabbi Kushner, like Victor Frankl, writes with the authority of one who has suffered senseless events. Kushner offers the provocative notion that perhaps God is not in charge of everything—that some things just happen.

Now, I had gotten clear the idea that some suffering, like being gunned down in a senseless school shooting, resulted from the freely chosen acts of others. We are a self-destructive species. But I struggled with things like my sisters' birth defects. Kushner suggests that indeed such things just happen. I have struggled with this concept ever since I first read it in the early 1980s. Where, then, is God in the midst of such suffering? Clearly present, say Kushner and others. But as a comfort, not as a cause.

What I have begun to realize is that I let go reluctantly of the notion of a God who is all-powerful, who is responsible for everything. There is a part of me that wants it all to make sense, even if I don't like the answer. I cling sometimes to the notion Harold Kushner rejects. He suggests one view that posits life to be like the backside of a knitted wall hanging. We see various strands of string. But God sees the other side, the meaningful pattern. I cling to a hope that this is so.

And so some fifty years later I still don't know why my sisters were born with spina bifida. I don't know why my parents were dealt such blows. I'm not even sure where God is or was in the midst of all this. What I do know is that going quietly does not work for me. I take great comfort from my friend Job.

Job, you may remember, was a good and decent man who suffered as a result of a deal made between God and Satan. He lost everything. Worse yet, his buddies turned on him, telling him he'd surely sinned or simply wasn't praying hard enough. Job clearly suffered senselessly. And he blamed God for the suffering. In fact, he was angry with God. He even demanded that God show up and make an accounting of himself. Granted, God resorted to some special effects and put Job in his place. But God never punished Job for being angry.

I have been told by some very good people to not question God. Sorry, but that doesn't work for me. Whatever God I am able to believe in has to be one who will allow me to be angry. I once read a beautiful book by Pierre Wolff titled *May I Hate God?* (Paulist Press, 1983). Wolff's answer is a resounding "Yes." He draws a beautiful metaphor. We are taught God is a loving Father/Mother. What loving parent, if his/her child were angry with him/her, would not want to hear about it? "Tell me what you're upset about. Let's talk about it. See if we can't straighten things out. Don't withdraw into silence!" This may be a God I can approach.

REFLECTION: Have you ever been angry with God? Write about it.

On Prayer

A second spiritual theme emerged in my preschool years. My mother was a great believer in prayer. Her prayer was almost entirely selfless. I nonetheless got the idea that I could pray for things for myself. Stuff. Thus, when I was four or five, and after being turned down by my parents, I prayed for a pony.

My parents, mainly my mother, had tried reasoning. We didn't have a back yard to keep a pony in, she would say. Or it would cost too much for upkeep. I was not to be deterred. I began to pray for a pony for Christmas.

My mother prayed a lot. She prayed for ill relatives. She prayed for missionaries. She prayed for the conversion of Russia. She prayed for my brother and me and then, after I was married and a father, for my wife and children. She had a deep belief in the power of prayer.

I can remember an early doubt I had about prayer. It had to do with two Catholic schools playing each other in some sporting event. Did God choose sides? Was the winning school a reflection of better praying? Later it occurred to me to wonder whether God was particularly interested in the outcome of an athletic competition.

Someone once said that at deathbeds and in foxholes there are many unanswered prayers. This issue of prayer obviously overlaps with my struggle about suffering, because unanswered prayers, according to some, reflect God's will. And, as Garth Brooks sings, sometimes God does indeed seem to know what he/she is doing.

But I have also dealt with many who prayed incessantly for a miracle only to lose a loved one to something like cancer, whereas someone else's family member recovers. Is there a trick here? Some sort of incantation that, if I figure it out, gets my prayers answered? Sadly, many persons in such a situation blame themselves, lamenting, "Perhaps I didn't pray hard enough or correctly." I have to reject the notion that there is a special formula or fervor that makes prayer work but that we have to guess at the formula. Such a God would be a cruel one.

What I have learned is that some people have a marvelous capacity to accept unanswered prayers calmly and without bitterness. I truly admire this. It reflects a depth of belief in God, in God's benevolence, and in God's will. But my heart aches when I listen to a very good woman say that, because her child died, this must mean that she did not pray correctly or that the sum total of her past sins canceled out any chance of her prayers being answered.

Do I still pray? In general, yes. I pray for good things for my wife and children. I pray when I am afraid. (Remember there are no atheists in foxholes!) And I have learned that prayers of gratitude help me feel more at peace. I don't pray much about money matters anymore because I really don't think God is interested in money problems. If anything, God is probably wary of money matters. Rich people don't like to be reminded of what Jesus had to say about their chances of getting into heaven.

And if you haven't guessed by now, no, I did not get my pony.

REFLECTION: What role has prayer played in your life? What types of experiences have you had? And what about unanswered prayers?

On Thinking and Doubting

When I began high school in 1962, the faint rumblings of change were just beginning to be felt within the Catholic Church. Some elements of tradition, however, were still evident. One of these traditions was the value and power of an education by Jesuits.

The Society of Jesus was founded by a warrior and had developed a strong tradition of intellectual acuity and educational excellence. Two goals were clearly elucidated in the Jesuit philosophy of education: learn to study and learn to think. The Jesuits, I found, were not afraid to think. It was the Jesuits who taught me that there is no such thing as a dangerous idea.

My history of behavior problems did not evaporate in the presence of Jesuits, although they were tempered somewhat by rumors that our headmaster Father Bernard McIlhenny was a former Golden Gloves champion. But there was a certain pride involved with attending the local Jesuit high school.

These men by and large fit a pre-Vatican II picture of priests—tough men, many of whom were veterans of cither the Second World War or the Korean War. Priests of this era were more like football coaches. Many of them also were hard drinkers.

In September of 1962, I entered the local Jesuit High school and met some men who would profoundly affect my journey. During my first year, our religion class was taught by John FitzPatrick, SJ, a man who, according to rumor, had been a paratrooper. Father FitzPatrick early on proposed a notion that was then truly shocking: He suggested that we not take everything literally that was in the *Baltimore Catechism*.

The *Baltimore Catechism* was the mainstay of Catholic education at that time. It presented basic truths of the Catholic faith in question-and-answer format, thus communicating a certain "black-and-white" flavor. Questions and answers were to be memorized, then recited by rote upon request. This was the backbone of religious education. Questions and ponderings were not encouraged. Everything in the *Baltimore Catechism* was to be simply accepted "on faith."

Father FitzPatrick's directive was more than a little alarming. He pointed out, for example, that the discussion of the effects of "impure acts" was just a little inaccurate, and was so forthright as to tell us pubescent boys that, despite what the catechism said, masturbation did not cause brain damage or insanity. This nowadays can seem ludicrous, but such were the scare tactics of the day. But at Father FitzPatrick's suggestion, the door was open for me to question, even to have doubts. If things in the *Baltimore Catechism* were to be examined, even questioned....This was truly a revolutionary notion.

Doubts, you see, had been discouraged, even viewed as weak, if not downright sinful. But here was a man of God encouraging me to think about what I believed. This mustard seed of wisdom would in time allow me not only to have doubts but also to welcome them.

REFLECTION: Have there been times of doubting during your spiritual journey? With what doubts have you struggled?

Somewhere during these years, I noticed more clearly Saint Thomas the Apostle, a man who became one of my spiritual mentors. Many look down on Thomas, viewing him as inferior because he longed for a sign to bolster his faith. The story is basically that Jesus had risen from the dead, but Thomas would not believe it unless he was able to touch Jesus' wounds. Jesus appears, Thomas sees him, and Jesus offers Thomas the opportunity to touch his wounds. Thomas is appropriately humble. Jesus then adds particular praise for those who believe without a sign. But he never condemns Thomas!

Some years later, I saw in this story Jesus' deep love for Thomas. Have you ever suffered a scarring injury or gone through a significant surgery? Would you share your scars with someone, much less invite someone to touch them? This is a very intimate communication. Yet Jesus extended this offer to Thomas so that he might be more secure in his beliefs. Jesus loved Thomas this much!

So for me, Thomas became a source of hope in the midst of my doubts. Maybe those of us who struggle to believe are not lost.

I have always admired people of simple faith. These are people who are not dogmatic, who do not project a "better than" attitude regarding their beliefs. These people of simple faith are humble folk who do not impose their beliefs on others but who conduct themselves in accord with a few straightforward beliefs that, by and large, they do not question. I truly envy such simple faith. I do not use the term simple to imply some lack of intellectual power. Rather, it is meant to imply a lack of complications, for I have also seen that the dark side of a thoughtful approach to faith can be a good deal of confusion and needless complexity.

REFLECTION: Have you known people of simple faith? What impact have they had on your journey?

During my high school years, the full impact of Vatican II was being felt in that priests and sisters began a fairly massive exodus from their religious lives into the world of the laity. In Jesuit training, men would serve a period of time as a "scholastic" during which they would teach and live in a religious community. They were, however, several years away from ordination. Of the fifteen or so scholastics I knew during my high school years, only three would ever be ordained. One of the priests who left during that time was actually the ranking Jesuit of the Maryland province.

His departure planted a question in many minds: "Maybe I can leave. Maybe I can be just as good a person in another lifestyle."

I had not yet parted company with the idea of becoming a priest. In fact, during my senior year, I applied to and was accepted by the Holy Cross fathers. I have to admit that I was drawn to them in part because they were affiliated with Notre Dame. But I had visited their seminary in Massachusetts and was drawn to the quiet and to the intense spiritual focus. The vocations director, Father Frank Gartland, was also an old-school type of priest, a good spiritual man who enriched my journey. Unfortunately, I also had exposure to the emerging dark side of celibacy at that seminary when a seminarian with whom I was rooming tried to molest me.

However, I continued to be exposed to positive role models of priesthood. I first learned of Father Charles Dismas Clark through the film *The Hoodlum Priest.* Father Clark worked in St. Louis on behalf of the incarcerated and developed a halfway-house movement for them. His story allowed me to fully embrace Saint Dismas the Good Thief. Dismas became my second significant saint.

According to legend, Dismas was crucified with Christ. While they were dying, as recorded by Saint Luke, another criminal began to mock Jesus. Dismas cut him short, then turned to Jesus and asked to be remembered. Jesus uttered incredible words: "Today you will be with me in paradise." This story of Dismas has stood ever since as a beacon of hope for me and for others. I have, over the years, given religious medals of Saint Dismas to those waging special wars against poor self-esteem. Dismas had truly hit bottom yet was promised eternal reward. This ought to encourage all of us.

The other facet of faith that paralleled the permission to doubt was the emphasis Jesuits place on thinking. I was taught, then encouraged, to think about what I believed. This may not seem like much of an insight, but in those days (and to some extent still) there were elements in various organized religions that stated that good faith does not question but merely accepts in a childlike manner.

Most religious traditions are replete with thinkers—men and women who analyzed the tenets of their faith either to understand them better or to attempt to explain them more clearly to others. Sometimes thinkers are condemned and persecuted. Witness the likes of Galileo. Thinkers tend to be attacked when the fruit of their thinking challenges the party line. Teilhard de Chardin is a case in point. De Chardin was a brilliant anthropologist-priest (a Jesuit!) whose complex theories of evolution were roundly condemned in the 1940s and 1950s with de Chardin being silenced. Subsequent to his death, his works eventually were reconsidered, and today he is regarded as a mystic and visionary.

I do understand why some authorities discourage thinking about one's beliefs, for if you think, then you may question. And if you question, you may reject. Or, at the very least, you may discover that you really don't understand what something means.

REFLECTION: Are there any religious beliefs to which you aspire but about which you rarely think? List them.

There are many tenets of my Catholicism that I now realize I don't understand. Haven't the foggiest. Body and Blood of Christ? Don't have a clue! This doesn't mean, however, that I automatically reject such notions. Only that I need to think about them.

Thinking, too, challenges us to lay claim to what we believe. Thinking, in essence, allows us to confront the question, "Why do you believe what you believe?"

REFLECTION: How do you approach such a question at this time?

Alcohol consumption became an increasing part of my life in high school. In those days it was a sign of manhood to be able to consume huge amounts of beer. Given that I was an otherwise insecure soul, I developed some skill at this. By the time I was a senior, some of my friends and I were drinking like alcoholics.

In my last two years of high school, I was also greatly influenced by Father John Herrity, SJ. Father Herrity had originally been our math teacher, but by the time I was a senior he taught religion and also mentored the sodality. Sodalities to this point were social-service organizations in many Catholic schools. Father Herrity introduced, however, a revolutionary idea. Why not join our sodality with that of the local Catholic all-girls school? Father Herrity, it seemed, sensed the twisted view of women that our education gave us and took it upon himself to try to offset that. So the halls of our high school rang with the voices of girls.

Beyond this, Father Herrity had the courage to guide us into areas of thought clearly at odds with Catholic thinking. During these years, a controversy evolved known as the "Death of God" controversy. Philosophers questioned the validity or necessity of the concept of God. Rather than blindly condemning such thinking, Father Herrity encouraged us to examine it! Thus, I found myself reading Friedrich Nietzsche. Not that I understood him, but this exposure did introduce me to the notion that ideas were to be examined, that we should avoid what is known in Alcoholics Anonymous circles as "contempt prior to investigation."

REFLECTION: Have you encountered ideas in your spiritual journey that you were afraid to examine? What "dangerous ideas" did you face head-on?

On Loving

The significant event of my freshman year in college occurred in the spring. I knew of the University Players, the
school drama group with a reputation for cast parties. I was too shy
to try out for their fall production, even though I had done some
plays in high school. However, one March afternoon I noticed a
sign announcing auditions for a spring production of *Spoon River
Anthology*, a stage version of the poems of Edgar Lee Masters. I
had read many of these poems in high school and truly loved
them. This I could not pass up. When I came to auditions, the
faculty director, a kind and gentle spirit named Bernard McGurl,
greeted me warmly. He had judged me in a high school speech
contest and was pleased to see me. I was cast and spent the next
four years doing a variety of roles.

Art has played a major role in my spiritual journey. Directions,
even answers, which my Catholicism did not provide, were un-
covered through art. Music has also enriched my path, Certain
songs still have a way of bypassing my intellectualism and tapping
into my feelings. Hymns such as "Be Not Afraid" and "You Are
Near" have been a source of great comfort during times of trial.
Some travelers clearly benefit from the visual arts. Henri Nouwen's
biographer portrays Nouwen's work with various religious icons
to enhance his journey. For me, standing before Dali's *The Last
Supper* was a deep spiritual moment.

REFLECTION: What works of art have enriched your spiritual
journey? How often do you allow yourself to make contact
with these works?

The significance of theater was not the roles or the parties but the fact that, through theater, I met the young woman who was to become my wife.

Learning about loving has been a critical facet of my spiritual journey. Tending toward introversion, I have needed to be challenged to explore intimacy and vulnerability. My wife is an extrovert and at ease with her feelings. As such, our life together has not been dull.

Saint Paul says it clearly: "God is love, and he who abides in love abides in God and God in him." Yet we seem to think of spiritual journeys in individual terms. I would argue that one's history of and experience with loving intimate relationships is a key facet of the spiritual autobiography.

REFLECTION: As simple as it may sound, make a list of the people in your life whom you love and/or have loved.

What kind of love are we talking about here? Don't limit yourself by definitions. List whatever comes to you as loving, be it deep platonic love, head-over-heels puppy love, passionate love, parental love, or whatever form loving has taken in your life. All the loving you've experienced has been instructive on the spiritual path.

The topic of love has intrigued poets, philosophers, and psychologists for centuries and continues to be explored from multiple angles. As a guide, however, for assessing just how we are doing as far as being lovers is concerned, I find great help from the late Morton Kelsey.

Father Kelsey was a gentle man who wrote extensively on the interface of psychology and spirituality. Though I only met him once, I regard him as a spiritual mentor. In his book *Companions on the Inner Way: The Art of Spiritual Guidance* (Crossroad: New York, 1983), Father Kelsey explores what he sees as thirteen facets of human loving. I use his thoughts here to propose an inventor to be used for self-examination. Approach it not from a position of judgment but from a position of growth. We all, each and every one of us, saint or sinner, can stand to become even better lovers.

REFLECTION: Work on the following Inventory of Loving.

1. Have I made a conscious commitment to become a loving person? Is becoming a loving person even something I am interested in? Where does it fall on my list of priorities? If it is not my first priority, everything that comes before it will impact and limit my capacity to love. If, for example, money is my priority, then the pursuit of money may take precedence over the experience of love.

2. To what degree does my spiritual world reflect self-discipline? It is ironic to consider that something as seemingly spontaneous as loving would require a degree of self-discipline, yet we also know that the acquisition of a certain trait or outcome, like physical fitness, requires consistent repetition of a certain course of action (see Patterson, Richard B., *Becoming a Modern Contemplative: A Psychospiritual Model for Personal Growth*, Loyola University Press: Chicago, 1995).

3. How well do I love myself? This, I believe, is one of the great challenges of loving. Time and again I have counseled persons of service—therapists, priests and sisters, persons working in social justice, physicians. Without exception, these persons give freely of love and compassion yet judge themselves harshly. I remember counseling with a priest who faulted himself along certain lines. He sat berating himself and I asked him, "Tell me, when someone comes to you and confesses those sins, is this how you respond?" He was horrified, saying, "I would never say that to a penitent." So to assess myself as a lover, I need to examine how well I treat myself physically, mentally, emotionally, and spiritually. Do I treat my body gently or do I abuse it? Do I affirm myself or pass judgment? Do I place myself in needless stress or do I allow myself experiences that give me joy? Is my spirituality

filled with fear or with celebration? (See also Patterson, Richard B., *Encounters With Angels: Psyche and Spirit in the Counseling Situation*, Loyola University Press: Chicago, 1992, chapter 8.)

4. How well do I listen? One of the finest gifts my daughter Becky ever gave me was in the midst of an argument. As I was berating her about something, she cried out in frustration, "Dad, you're not listening to me!" She was right. I became so focused on control and being right that I was shutting her out. As psychologist Carl Rogers (see, for example, *On Becoming a Person*, Mariner Books: New York, 1995) illustrated so beautifully, listening is not passive. We are involved. We express verbally and nonverbally that we are paying attention. We feed back what we are hearing to ensure accuracy. We do not interrupt.

5. How do I deal with my feelings of hurt? Withholding of negative feelings can give rise to resentments and/or acts of explosiveness and vengeance. Yet most of us hold on to such feelings, perhaps out of fear, perhaps out of payback. Sharing one's feelings of hurt is a risk. We make ourselves vulnerable to the person who hurt us. Thus, we need to evaluate the wisdom of sharing negative feelings based on the relationship's track record for dealing with them. In other words, even if this person hurt me, do I trust him/her?

6. How well do I do love those closest to me? Many of us, especially in the helping and healing professions, pour out compassion to others but then treat our own loved ones poorly, taking out our frustrations on them or expecting special treatment because we spend such long hours being of service. To see how I am doing with loving, I need to look no further than my own family. How affirming and encouraging am I of them? How much and how often do I encourage the growth of each one? How available do I make myself? How much do I share?

7. How hospitable and welcoming am I to strangers? This does not mean that I should give money to every street person or invite

him or her home for dinner. But it does means that I should not pass judgment on each street corner. Closer to home, there are constant opportunities to make others feel welcome. Do I introduce myself to the new neighbor? If I belong to a club, do I greet newcomers or do I stay with those I know?

8. Finally, we come to the greatest challenge to loving—the love of one's enemies. Here we need to recall Kelsey's observation that enemies are not only those whom we do not like but those who might not like us. (*op. cit.*, p. 207). It may be helpful to first make a list of your enemies. Can you look at each name and identify something about that person that you admire? Do you gossip or condone gossip about each person on your list? Which ones are targets of resentments?

One-to-one long-term relationships may be one of the most powerful schools in loving. For in long-term relationships, we experience all the challenges of tolerance and acceptance. We experience the temptation to take good relationships for granted, to not work on them constantly. Our "Shadow" side displays itself with alarming regularity.

Psychiatrist Carl Jung provided us with the great insight of the Shadow. This is a part of one's personality to which we do not like to admit. It is that within us which is potentially destructive. Our potential to violence, to selfishness, even to unbridled lust resides within our Shadow. The more we deny something within ourselves, the stronger it becomes within our Shadow.

But the effort to push the Shadow away does not work. It presses to be faced and integrated, a truly daunting task. It shows up when we least want it. And it especially shows up in our most intimate relationships, both as unpleasant, seemingly foreign modes of behavior and, more often, as projections.

REFLECTION: What experiences have you had with "falling in love?" How did they turn out?

Bridges From Psyche to Spirit

I left the army in 1979, choosing to open a private practice in the Southwest desert. My Catholic faith was in a pretty shabby state but I was once again motivated to take a course in self-study. I began to read about other religions and found myself especially drawn to Zen Buddhism. Perhaps it was the anti-intellectual flavor of Zen that called to me. In any case, I read books that had a powerful impact. In particular, *Zen Mind, Beginner's Mind* by S. Suzuki (Weatherhill, 1997) and *Zen and the Art of Motorcycle Maintenance* by Robert Pirsig (Bantam Books, 1984) seemed to speak to me. Early on, I had an affirming dream. I was running with Salvador Minuchin, a famous family therapist whom I admired. Minuchin turned to me in the dream and said, "You're on the right track with your interest in Zen."

I'd grown up with the concept of the "One True Religion." Of course, many other religions view themselves as the O.T.R. In any case, this belief in the O.T.R. included a suspiciousness of other faiths. Dialogue with clients of various faiths had begun to erode this notion.

My son, Andy, philosopher that he is, once suggested that religions were simply different opinions. Are they simply a waste of time? I believe that it is arrogant to ignore the teachings of other spiritual travelers. My own stumbling journey has been greatly enriched by Zen, by Judaism and Jewish mysticism. I resonated to the words of Rabbi Lawrence Kushner that each person has a Torah unique to that person. "Some seem to know their Torah very early. Others spend their whole lives stammering, shaping, and rehearsing them. Some are long, some short. Some are intricate and poetic, others are only a few words, and still others can only be spoken through gesture and example. But every soul has a Torah" (*God Was in This Place and I, I Did Not Know*, Jewish lights: Woodstock, VT, p. 177).

REFLECTION: If you were raised in a religious tradition, what facets have you held onto? How has your walk been enriched by other approaches to the spiritual journey?

At the time I was drawn to Zen, I cannot say that I knew for sure what was drawing me. I can say in retrospect that Buddhism has much to say about suffering, which was one of my central struggles. I can also say that, in the midst of addiction, I needed to begin thinking about attachments and letting go. Zen Buddhism seemed to provide something I needed without my knowing that I needed it. These experiences provided me with a beginning understanding of the idea of grace.

REFLECTION: As you reflect on your journey, do you see any points where you were provided with something you needed, even though you might not have known it at the time?

I suppose that I was ironically drawn to the somewhat anti-intellectual flavor of Zen Buddhism. Zen seemed to encourage me to "let go" of my great need to understand something. In its own way, Zen seemed to suggest that the more I felt I understood something spiritual, the further away I was from the truth. In Zen terms, "He who says does not know. He who knows does not say." Thus, Zen provided needed balance to what the Jesuits taught me about thinking.

Zen also helped me appreciate the paradoxical side of God. In the Gospels, Jesus often spoke in paradoxical terms ("The first shall be last and the last shall be first," for example). Zen provided a rich appreciation of paradox. Also enriching was the Buddhist notion of the Five Wonderful Precepts—"reverence for life, generosity, responsible sexual behavior, speaking and listening deeply, and ingesting only wholesome substances" (Hanh, *ibid.*, p. 91). During this time I also was exposed to Taoism. The Taoist notion of complementary polarities (Yin-Yang) also held powerful appeal. It helped me see that virtue, for example, was meaningless without my appreciation of sin. That light only made sense in relation to darkness. This greatly impacted my moral thinking. Several interpreters of Taoism pointed out that God might only have meaning in relation to not-God. And in true Taoist manner, Carl Jung spoke of God's Dark Side.

I continued to struggle with trying to find some sort of bridge which could encompass both my psychological background and my spiritual yearnings. I consulted with the local Catholic diocesan marriage tribunal run by Joe Nelen, a gentle-spirited, brilliant priest. Over lunch one day, I shared my yearnings and Joe mentioned two writers to me—John A. Sanford and Morton Kelsey. I immediately went to a local bookstore and found a copy of John Sanford's *The Kingdom Within* (Harper-SanFrancisco, 1987). I also came across Henri Nouwen's *The Wounded Healer* (Image Books, 1979), and picked up a copy of Morton Kelsey's *Companions on the Inner Way* (Crossroad, 1983). A new world opened up to me!

Slowly, the bridge took form. Sanford's *The Kingdom Within* approaches the gospels from the perspective of Jungian psychiatry and suggests that Jesus' parables have an inner meaning and relevance to the psychological journeys and struggles of each one of us. Sanford is not attempting to psychologize Jesus. Rather, he is exploring one particular approach to tapping the richness of Jesus' sayings. In particular, he opens up the Jungian approach to use dreams as a tool for understanding Jesus' sayings.

I had studied dreams previously when I was seeing Ramon. But the works of Sanford spoke powerfully to the value of dreams on the spiritual path. I have tried to listen to my dreams since then. Often they are puzzling and obtuse. Sometimes they are disturbing. But if I take the time to listen, they can be a powerful guide on the journey.

A brief example. Somewhere during this time, I had a dream wherein I confronted an SS officer who was in some way jeopardizing some children. I drove him away and even pardoned him as he was leaving.

After waking from this dream, I felt rather heroic! But later it occurred to me that the SS officer was also a reflection of myself. Now I didn't feel quite so heroic.

The Jungian theory, however, suggested that this dream was trying, through the figure of the SS officer, to point me toward some aspect of my Shadow side with which I needed to make contact. After some reflection, it occurred to me that the SS officer might represent self-discipline, a quality I sorely lack. Sadly, he represents more than that—my own capacity for cruelty among other things. But he did help me find some capacity for self-discipline, which in turn has made it possible for me to write.

But it was Nouwen's image of the "wounded healer" that truly haunted me. Nouwen, I would learn, did not create the image. It is an image that can be found in numerous cultures and is at the heart of shamanic religions practice. But Nouwen put the image in terms I could grasp.

A wounded healer is one who has suffered and been wounded but has faced his/her wounds, done some healing, and then draws upon those wounds as a resource for bringing healing to others. It is also an image that lies at the root of the current self-help movement. I felt drawn to it yet had limited insight into the core of my own woundedness.

Nouwen challenges us to embrace our own wounds as a resource to truly connect with others. Often we shrink from our own pain, wanting to find comfort without feeling the pain. Such avoidance has a great price tag. It becomes very difficult for us to be truly empathic, to genuinely feel one another's pain. And it becomes virtually impossible to grow.

I would like to claim that the first time I read Nouwen's *The Wounded Healer*, the clouds parted and I saw the light. But this wouldn't be true. The book struck a chord, but I didn't fully answer. In retrospect, I am reminded of the story of the preacher and the flood. The floodwaters were rising and a truck came along to take the preacher to high ground, but he refused, saying, "My prayers will save me." Then a boat came along as the waters continued to rise but again he turned them down, professing, "My prayers will save me!" Finally, a helicopter offered to pick him off his rooftop. But again he refused. And he drowned. Needless to say, when he met his Lord, he was a bit upset. But the Lord said. "Well, I sent you help three times and you turned me down each time!"

So I was still insisting that I could fix my own messes without any help.

REFLECTION: Have there been points in your journey when help crossed your path but you turned it down?

Our Image of God

Perhaps you can remember where you first heard about God. I cannot. I have a vague memory of attending Mass at some early point in my life. I vaguely recall being bored and restless. One of my earliest memories centers on the Bible we had in our house. It had reproductions of classical paintings, including one of Abraham about to slaughter his son. I found those pictures both horrifying and fascinating. I didn't understand anything about the tricky theological issues inherent in that event. (Personally, I often wonder what the conversation coming down from the mountain was like. "What was that all about, Pa?"—something along those lines.) So I'm fairly certain that my early image of God was indeed the stereotypic bearded Anglo-Saxon character with a rather fierce look in his eyes.

REFLECTION: What are some of your early spiritual memories? What was your image of God when you were little?

My own image of God had been fairly static and negative until I underwent therapy. Then I began to experience a healing side of God. Through John Sanford's *The Kingdom Within* I saw that God could be a profound and insightful psychologist. And the God that I met the first day of my sobriety was clearly a God of grace and miracles.

But the God of my understanding that evolved during the 1980s still had residual qualities of the God of my childhood. I still feared going to hell. I still had some mixed-up notions about what sin is. And the God of that time was clearly a man.

Thomas Merton once wrote that our image of God tells us more about ourselves than about God himself (see *New Seeds of*

Contemplation, New Directions: New York, 1961, p. 1). The God that I have believed in reflected my fears and my great struggles with letting go. Even in recovery, I might have stayed stuck with that image; however, in 1987 I attended a workshop given by Matthew Linn, Dennis Linn, and Sheila Fabricant. These gentle, kind souls introduced an idea that to me was revolutionary—the idea of God as female. This possibility was introduced within the context of exploring the notion that the image of God that we have acquired is mediated by human beings, especially our fathers, and therefore may be in need of some healing. The doorway the Linns and Ms. Fabricant proposed was to image God as a loving mother.

The image of God as loving mother had simply never occurred to me! The imagery I experienced was of a loving, nurturing God, the kind of God whom in many ways I'd grown to long for. This healing essentially allowed me to break free from the confining image of God as a man. This in turn allowed me to image God in many ways, not just as a woman.

REFLECTION: What is your image of God at this point in your life? Who are some of the people who influenced this image?

I had learned through AA that I would benefit spiritually if I developed my own understanding of God. But it was not until this workshop that I realized how confining the image was that I'd grown up with.

The second major shift in my image of God came more slowly. Influenced by Teilhard de Chardin and by Jungian analyst Fritz Kunkel, I began to sense a God whose acts of creation did not stop after seven days. I came to believe in a God who continues to create and looks to each of us to participate in this creation.

Teilhard was both priest and scientist. He did not automatically reject the concept of evolution. In fact, he developed an astounding theory that viewed evolution from a spiritual perspective and viewed God as actively involved in the process of evolution. In essence, he viewed creation as ongoing. This notion has further been explored from a variety of perspectives. Fritz Kunkel wrote about creation continuing from an intrapsychic perspective (*Creation Continues*, Word Books: Waco, TX, 1973). The immanence of God's creation runs through Ian Bradley's suggestion of God as green and therefore active in all of creation (*God Is Green: Ecology for Christians*, Image: New York, 1990). Charles Cummings, another ecological theologian, gives us an interesting twist on evolution, saying evolution is another term for the ongoing creative activity of God (see *Eco-Spirituality: Toward a Reverent Life*, Paulist: Mahwah, NJ, 1991, p. 10). And God's active creative presence is found in the rediscovery of the centuries-old Celtic Christianity. (See, for example, Anthony Duncan, *The Elements of Celtic Christianity*, Element Books: Shaftesbury, Doset, Great Britain, 1992.)

Participating in God's creation can be an intimidating idea. It at least makes sense that we should not get in the way. Thus, the notion of God's creation continuing has had direct impact on my beliefs about just how important it is to pursue a lifestyle of peace. To do otherwise would seem to interfere with the manner in which my neighbor participates in God's creation.

I've come to believe something else about us as humans. Some years ago my friend Dick Park invited me to participate in a workshop on journaling. As an experiment, I decided I would present a "mini-course" on writing poetry and then invite participants to share their poems. At that time the result was surprising. Many participants produced and shared poems. Many of the poems shared were quite profound. Beyond that, many of the participants were pleasantly surprised to discover this inner poet. I have done this exercise often since then and always with the same result—profound poems and pleasantly surprised participants. This pattern has convinced me that one of the ways in which we participate in God's creation is by embracing and expressing our artistic creativity.

As Julia Cameron writes in *The Artists' Way* (J.P. Tarcher, 1992), one of the greatest impediments to our creativity is the judgment we pass on the products of our creative efforts. This tends to be fear-based because the products of our creativity are very personal and so, when we contemplate sharing them, we become afraid. I know in my case with each of the books I've written, I always was excited to receive the first box of books. But upon opening the box, each time I felt a little panic. I realized that the publication of the book made me feel vulnerable to criticism, to judgment.

There are so many ways we can participate in God's creation. Writing poems is certainly one way. But there are so many others. The arts as we typically think of them. Cooking. Gardening. Designing a room. Playing with a child. The possibilities are vast, for the creative God is a God of abundance.

REFLECTION: How do you express your creativity? If you have no creative expressions, what gets in the way?

Conclusion

I summarize where I am in my journey at this point with these observations:

1. I seem to be rediscovering something of value in the roots of my Catholicism.
2. I see value in simple faith and in stoic faith.
3. I continue to find great value in what I understand of Zen Buddhism. Thoughts on suffering and on attachments have been especially impactful.
4. My journey has been enriched by Jewish theologians and mystics.
5. I have major issues with the organization of the Catholic Church. While I have encountered some truly wonderful people serving the Church, I find the organization to be focused heavily on power and to be sexually neurotic.
6. I continue to need to work on "horizontal spirituality," that is, spirituality that involves community and service.
7. I continue to wrestle with serious doubts about the impact of prayer and the existence and nature of an afterlife. I continue to experience powerful outcomes to my prayers yet continue, like Saint Thomas the Apostle, to look for signs.
8. I am humbled to see just how much anger and outcry has been a part of my relationship with the God of my understanding. He/She has been very patient.

REFLECTION: Can you summarize where you are spiritually right now?

Rabbi David Wolpe sums up well what I believe to be true at this point: that the search for faith in one's life is a battle, wonderful and bitterly disappointing. But part of being human is asking the most important questions that confront us, asking them again and again, not letting them go until we figure out what it means to be a human being, why we were put here, whether we were put here for any reason at all (*The Healer of Shattered Hearts: A Jewish View of God*, Penguin: New York, 1990, pp. 20–21).

I have a hunch. Is it possible, as I crash around in the bushes seeking God, that he/she is standing right nearby the entire time, waiting patiently for me? Perhaps the day will come when I finally turn around and learn once and for all what C.S. Lewis saw years ago: So it was you all along. (See *The Inspirational Writings of C.S. Lewis*, p. 288).

REFLECTION: Where would you like to be spiritually a year from now?

Annotated Bibliography

What follows are some suggestions for further reading. Included are readings on some but not all of the topics we covered.

INTRODUCTION TO SPIRITUAL AUTOBIOGRAPHIES

Amy Mandeleker and Elizabeth Powers, eds. *Pilgrim Souls: A Collection of Spiritual Autobiography* (Touchstone; New York, 1999). This is an excellent survey of spiritual autobiographies, excerpts ranging from Socrates and King David to Flannery O'Connor and Annie Dillard. It would be hard not to find a kindred soul among the excerpts.

A Selection of Spiritual Autobiographies

Thomas Merton, *The Seven Storey Mountain* (Harvest Books: Orlando, FL, 1999). This may be the best known of spiritual autobiographies and is the story of Father Merton's journey from man of the world to Trappist monk.

C.S. Lewis, *Mere Christianity* (Harper SanFrancisco, 2001). Lewis has certainly become one of the most popular spiritual writers. This work portrays his intellectual awakening to the tenets of Christianity.

Henri Nouwen, *Seeds of Hope: A Henri Nouwen Reader* (Doubleday: New York, 1997). Most of Father Nouwen's writings have strong autobiographical elements to them. This work provides an overview. Other works of his with strong autobiographical themes include *Road to Daybreak* and *The Inner Voice of Love* (Doubleday: New York, 1998).

Rick Bragg, *All Over But the Shoutin'* (Vintage Books: New York, 1998). This book might at first glance not seem to be the stuff of spirituality. But it includes Mr. Bragg's struggles with organized religion and most especially is a story of how his mother faced suffering with courage and dignity.

Anne Lamott, *Traveling Mercies: Some Thoughts on Faith* (Anchor Books: New York, 2000). Ms. Lamott shares her own journey in a most endearing manner. She gives hope to those of us who stumble and who have battled addiction.

Other favorite spiritual autobiographies have included Annie Dillard's *Pilgrim at Tinker Creek* (Harper Perennial: New York, 1998), Terry Tempest Williams' *Refuge* (Vintage Books: New York, 1992), Carl Jung's *Memories, Dreams, Reflections* (Vintage Books: New York, 1989), Loren Eiseley's *All the Strange Hours: The Excavation of a Life* (Bison Books: Omaha, NE, 2000), and Louise Fisher's collection of the writings of Mahatma Gandhi, *The Essential Gandhi: An Anthology of His Writings on His Life, Work and Ideas* (Vintage Books: New York, 1983).

On Suffering

The suggested readings here provided no answers but point toward good questions.

Viktor Frankl, *Man's Search for Meaning* (Washington Square Press: New York, 1998). This classic work provides the essentials of Frankl's theory on meaning as well as Frankl's experiential context for this theory. A more theoretical exploration of Frankl's theory of logotherapy can be found in his *The Doctor and the Soul* (Vintage Books: New York, 1986).

Harold Kushner, *When Bad Things Happen to Good People* (Avon: New York, 1997). Another classic exploration of making sense of suffering.

William Safire, *The First Dissident: The Book of Job in Today's Politics* (Random House: New York, 1993). Job is certainly one of the most interesting and ignored figures in sacred writings. Safire's examination of his story is thought-provoking and, for those of us who struggle with spiritual anger, comforting.

Bridges from Psychology to Spirituality and Back

Morton Kelsey, *Companions on the Inner Way* (Crossroad: New York, 1979). Written as a guide for spiritual direction, this book is valuable to anyone trying to accompany people on spiritual journeys. While written from a Christian perspective, its insights are ecumenical.

Henri Nouwen, *The Wounded Healer* (Image Books: New York, 1979). A good introduction to the archetype that is also an essential feature of the bridge.

Sheldon Kopp, *If You Meet the Buddha on the Road, Kill Him* (Bantam Books: New York, 1988). Many of Sheldon Kopp's writings are spiritual in nature with an emphasis on integrating Eastern thought into psychological practice. This book is one of his best known. Also recommended is *End to Innocence: Life Without Illusions* (Bantam Books: New York, 1983).